M000279031

THE MAN WHO LEFT HIS MARK

PETER KREEFT

The Man Who Left His Mark

~

How Mark's Gospel Answers Modern Questions

IGNATIUS PRESS   SAN FRANCISCO

Unless otherwise indicated, Scripture quotations are from Revised Standard Version of the Bible—Second Catholic Edition (Ignatius Edition). Copyright © 2006 National Council of the Churches of Christ in the United States of America. Used by permission. All rights reserved worldwide.

Cover image
Saint Mark the Evangelist (detail)
Emmanuel Tzanes (1610–1690)
Banaki Museum, Athens
Wikimedia Commons image

(*with a laptop*)

Cover design by Enrique J. Aguilar

© 2022 by Ignatius Press, San Francisco
All rights reserved
ISBN 978-1-62164-582-5 (PB)
ISBN 978-1-64229-244-2 (eBook)
Library of Congress Control Number 2022934002
Printed in the United States of America ∞

Introduction

Mark's Gospel is the quickest and "busiest" of the four: the Gospel for Americans.

One of its most frequently used words is "suddenly" or "immediately". This Gospel is a series of sudden shocks and surprises because that is how Jesus appeared to Mark and others who followed Him: as a series of sudden shocks and surprises. Following Christ—i.e., being a Christian—is more like following a car in a chase than like following a formula in an equation.

I designed this book to be a time machine: to sling you suddenly back twenty centuries so you can meet Jesus afresh. The means I use to that end is juxtaposing Jesus' answers with modern questions—a technique I began in *Letters to Jesus*, which was on Matthew's Gospel.

This is *not* a clever trick. It is neither clever nor a trick. It is not clever but simple, and it is not tricky but serious. For what could be more simple and more serious, more obvious and more important, than connecting up with Jesus, connecting His answers with our questions?

But beware: there are surprises in store for you if you get closer. Everyone who met Jesus was "amazed" (*thaumadzein*) at Him. You will not be the first exception—if you let Him speak to you.

In order to do that, in order to let Him speak to you, here is how to use this book:

1. First, cover up the answer, and think about the question for a minute, so that you can give *your* answer first and then compare Jesus' answer with your answer. That way, you will learn something about yourself as well as something about Him. Those are the two things that happened to everyone who met Him.

2. Ponder the answer Mark gives to each question for a minute before going on to the next question. My final comment on each Gospel answer is meant to help you to do that. This is not a Bible Quiz Book but a Ponder-Book.

1

What is the highest function of morality?

> MARK 1:2–3: "As it is written in Isaiah the prophet, 'Behold, I send my messenger before your face, who shall prepare your way; the voice of one crying in the wilderness: Prepare the way of the Lord, make his paths straight.'"

"The way to the Promised Land runs past [Mount] Sinai" (C. S. Lewis).

Morality in the soul is not Christ in the soul; but it is a red carpet for Christ to walk into the soul. Morality is for us all what John the Baptist was for the Jews.

2

What does Jesus give us that all the other prophets do not, if His message is the same as theirs?

> MARK 1:7–8: "[John] preached, saying, 'After me comes he who is mightier than I, the thong of whose sandals I am not worthy to stoop down and untie. I have baptized you with water; but he will baptize you with the Holy Spirit.'"

What other map-maker also gives you the fuel?

3

Different scholars, different philosophers, and different believers all have different answers to the question of who Jesus was.

How can I cut through the confusion and find the truth? To whom should I listen?

> MARK 1:11: "A voice came from heaven, 'You are my beloved Son; with you I am well pleased.'"

If Shakespeare told the scholars clearly what to make of his words, they would probably still go on squabbling and "interpreting".

4

When did angels and animals meet? Who can bring them (i.e., the whole cosmos) together?

> MARK 1:13: "And he was in the wilderness forty days, tempted by Satan; and he was with the wild beasts; and the angels ministered to him."

Jesus was where God designed man to be: between the animals and the angels—not where man designs God to be: between ideologies.

5

Where can I find a timely ethic for our age?

> MARK 1:14-15: "Jesus came into Galilee, preaching the gospel of God, and saying, 'The time is fulfilled . . . ; repent, and believe in the gospel.'"

Religion's most timely product is repentance. It is the door to a mansion—more, to a kingdom. And the door is open until time ends.

6

If I follow Christ, how will He change my business life?

MARK 1:16–17: "And passing along by the Sea of Galilee, he saw Simon and Andrew the brother of Simon casting a net in the sea; for they were fishermen. And Jesus said to them, 'Follow me and I will make you become fishers of men.'"

Things are for people, and people are for God. Using people is bad business; using God is bad religion. Using things for people is good business; serving God is good religion. Jesus taught His disciples to use all things to serve people into God.

7

How long does it take to become a Christian?

MARK 1:18: "And immediately they left their nets and followed him."

"There's no time like the present." In fact, there is no time *but* the present.

8

What is the difference between Jesus and a theologian?

MARK 1:22: "And they were astonished at his teaching, for he taught them as one who had authority, and not as the scribes."

The difference between Jesus and a theologian is like the difference between the ocean and an oceanographer.

9

What is the difference between Jesus and a psychologist?

> MARK 1:23–26: "And immediately there was in their synagogue a man with an unclean spirit; and he cried out, 'What have you to do with us, Jesus of Nazareth? Have you come to destroy us? I know who you are, the Holy One of God.' But Jesus rebuked him, saying, 'Be silent, and come out of him!' And the unclean spirit, convulsing him and crying with a loud voice, came out of him."

The difference between Jesus and a psychologist is like the difference between an operation and an office visit.

10

What is the difference between Jesus and a philosopher?

> MARK 1:27: "And they were all amazed, so that they questioned among themselves, saying, 'What is this? A new teaching! With authority he commands even the unclean spirits, and they obey him.'"

The difference between Jesus and a philosopher is like the difference between Superman and Woody Allen.

What happens after *Jesus saves and heals you?*

> MARK 1:30–31: "Now Simon's mother-in-law lay
> sick with a fever, and immediately they told him of
> her. And he came and took her by the hand and
> lifted her up, and the fever left her; *and she served
> them.*"

Jesus became our servant, not to make us masters, but
to make us servants.

*Which kind of life is better, a life of action or contemplation?
Crowds or solitude? City or country? Dialogue or silence?
Work or prayer?*

> MARK 1:32–35: "That evening, at sundown, they
> brought to him all who were sick or possessed with
> demons. And the whole city was gathered together
> about the door. And he healed many. . . . And in
> the morning, a great while before day, he rose and
> went out to a lonely place, and there he prayed."

Spiritual life and power are inhaled by prayer and
exhaled by work. Breathing requires both. (By the
way, the word for "spirit" and the word for "breath"
are identical in both Hebrew [*ruah*] and Greek [*pneu-
ma*].)

Why do we eventually get bored with everything? Why is everybody in the world, deep down, dissatisfied and discontent? Everybody is searching for something: What?

> MARK 1:37: "And they found him and said to him, 'Every one is searching for you.'"

If you gave any other answer to that question, please read 1 John 5:20–21: "*This* is the true God and eternal life. Little children, keep yourselves from idols."

14

Where is there a doctor who still makes house calls?

> MARK 1:38: "And he said to them, 'Let us go on to the next towns, that I may preach there also; for that is why I came out.'"

God is omnipresent because He moves infinitely fast from one house to the next.

15

If God is all-powerful, He can conquer any evil; and if He is all-good, He wills to conquer all evil. So what's going on? Does God lack power or goodness?

> MARK 1:40–42: "And a leper came to him begging him, and kneeling said to him, 'If you will, you can make me clean.' Moved with pity, he stretched out

his hand and touched him, and said to him, 'I will; be clean.' And immediately the leprosy left him, and he was made clean."

God lacks nothing of either power or goodness. *That* is clear. Sometimes He works quickly, sometimes slowly. His reasons for this strategy are *not* always clear. But they are always good.

16

What was Jesus' P.R. technique? How did He advertise Himself?

MARK 1:43–44: "And he [Jesus] sternly charged him [the miraculously healed leper], and sent him away at once, and said to him, 'See that you say nothing to any one; but go, show yourself to the priest. . . .' But he went out and began to talk freely about it, and to spread the news, so that Jesus could no longer openly enter a town, but was out in the country; and people came to him from every quarter."

Real fame is like real happiness: it is found only when it is not sought.

17

Does faith make you unaggressive and unpushy?

MARK 2:2–5: "And many were gathered together, so that there was no longer room for them, not even about the door; and he was preaching the word to them. And they came, bringing to him a paralytic carried by four men. And when they could not get near him because of the crowd, they removed the roof above him; and when they had made an opening, they let down the pallet on which the paralytic lay. And when Jesus saw their faith, he said to the paralytic, 'Child, your sins are forgiven.' "

Faith is humble but not polite. Like water or light, it always finds a way in.

18

Many different thinkers think many different things about who Jesus was. Who did He think He was?

MARK 2:5–7: "He said to the paralytic, 'Child, your sins are forgiven.' Now some of the scribes were sitting there, questioning in their hearts, 'Why does this man speak like this? It is blasphemy! Who can forgive sins but God alone?' "

A very good reason for joining Christ's Church (Body) is the one G. K. Chesterton gave: "To get my sins forgiven." And Who can do that?

19

Is there any hard empirical evidence, as distinct from abstract theological arguments, to prove that Jesus was not merely man but also God?

MARK 2:8–12 (see previous verses): "And immediately Jesus, perceiving in his spirit that they questioned like this within themselves, said to them, 'Why do you question like this in your hearts? Which is easier, to say to the paralytic, "Your sins are forgiven," or to say, "Rise, take up your pallet and walk"? But that you may know that the Son of man has authority on earth to forgive sins'—he said to the paralytic—'I say to you, rise, take up your pallet and go home.' And he rose, and immediately took up the pallet and went out before them all; so that they were all amazed and glorified God, saying, 'We never saw anything like this!' "

Saying "Your sins are forgiven" is easier, but *doing* it is harder, than healing a paralytic. Doing it took not just a word on paper but the Word on wood.

20

What do the beach and the I.R.S. have in common?

MARK 2:13–14: "He went out again beside the sea; and all the crowd gathered about him, and he taught them. And as he passed on, he saw Levi the son of Alphaeus sitting at the tax office, and he said to him, 'Follow me.' And he rose and followed him."

The deepest thing the beach and the I.R.S. have in common is the deepest thing all places have in common: Jesus meets us there.

Did Jesus come for everyone or only for some? If only some, what is my qualification, what makes me one of those for whom He came?

> MARK 2:15–17: "And as he sat at table in his house, many tax collectors and sinners were sitting with Jesus and his disciples; for there were many who followed him. And the scribes of the Pharisees, when they saw that he was eating with sinners and tax collectors, said to his disciples, 'Why does he eat with tax collectors and sinners?' And when Jesus heard it, he said to them, 'Those who are well have no need of a physician, but those who are sick; I came not to call the righteous, but sinners.'"

There are only two kinds of people in the world: saints, who know they are sinners, and sinners who think they are saints. Your entrance card to Doctor Jesus' office is your spiritual sickness; He treats only the needy. Do you qualify?

Is it not true that as Humanity "comes of age", it needs the simple, primitive religion of orthodox Christianity less and less? Isn't Christianity for the weak, the desperate, the failures, the losers? Look at all the poor, uneducated, ugly people who are Christians. Look at all the "beautiful people", the strong and mature and self-reliant people, who are not Christians. Does that not show something?—that Christianity is a crutch?

Yes, Christianity is a crutch. If you are not a cripple, you are not one of those for whom He came.

23

Is dieting not more reasonable than the traditional extremes of feasting and fasting?

MARK 2:18–20: "Now John's disciples and the Pharisees were fasting; and people came and said to him, 'Why do John's disciples and the disciples of the Pharisees fast, but your disciples do not fast?' And Jesus said to them, 'Can the wedding guests fast while the bridegroom is with them? As long as they have the bridegroom with them, they cannot fast. The days will come, when the bridegroom is taken away from them, and then they will fast in that day.'"

Chesterton says Christianity is like a bright checkerboard: very red and very white. "It has always had a healthy hatred of pink." Both feasting and fasting have what dieting lacks: passion.

24

What rips and rents and tears in our social fabric does Jesus mend? What frustrated desires of our psyches does he fulfill? Is he a prophet, a philosopher, a psychologist, a moralist, a sage, a social worker, a magician, a guru, a preacher, or an avatar?

MARK 2:21–22: "No one sews a piece of unshrunk cloth on an old garment; if he does, the patch tears away from it, the new from the old, and a worse tear is made. And no one puts new wine into old wineskins; if he does, the wine will burst the skins, and the wine is lost, and so are the skins; but new wine is for fresh skins."

We ask: "Are you the answer to my question?" He replies: "Are you the question to My answer?" Our desires must conform to His fulfillment, not His fulfillment to our desires and expectations and categories.

25

What is the point of morality, the purpose of moral laws?

MARK 2:27: "The sabbath was made for man, not man for the sabbath."

Without a vision of the nature and destiny of man, morality is slavish legalism or petty pragmatism.

26

What is the relation between Jesus and morality?

MARK 2:28: "The Son of man is lord even of the sabbath."

There is a Zen saying: "A finger is good for pointing at the moon, but woe to him who mistakes the finger for the moon." The point of the Law is to point to Christ (Gal 3:24); the point of Christ is not the Law. Christ is the bull's eye, the Law is the arrow.

27

What is the relation between moral law and life?

> MARK 3:1–4: "Again he entered the synagogue, and a man was there who had a withered hand. And they watched him, to see whether he would heal him on the sabbath, so that they might accuse him. And he said to the man who had the withered hand, 'Come here.' And he said to them, 'Is it lawful on the sabbath to do good or to do harm, to save life or to kill?' But they were silent."

Laws are for life, not life for the laws. That is why laws are more important than legalists think.

28

What is the greatest harm in legalism? If moral law is a good thing, how can it be so very bad to overdo a good thing?

> MARK 3:5: "And he looked around at them with anger, grieved at their hardness of heart."

The law is for the heart, not the heart for the law.

Can I imitate Christ even in my choice of vacations?

MARK 3:7: "Jesus withdrew with his disciples to the sea."

MARK 3:13: "And he went up on the mountain."

Seas and mountains are natural symbols of Heaven.

There have been many great and good men and women in history who have done enormous good and fought enormous evils—Socrates, Confucius, Muhammad, Lincoln, Gandhi—how was Jesus different? How could anyone see this difference?

MARK 3:11: "And whenever the unclean spirits saw him, they fell down before him and cried out, 'You are the Son of God.'"

"The kingdom of God does not consist in talk but in power" (1 Cor 4:20).

Did Jesus ever forbid anyone to tell the truth?

MARK 3:12: "And he strictly ordered them not to make him known."

When the right things are said by the wrong persons, the right things work for the wrong results.

32

How might a psychiatrist evaluate Christ?

> MARK 3:20–21: "And the crowd came together again, so that they could not even eat. And when his friends heard it, they went out to seize him, for they said, 'He is beside himself.'"

If Christ returned today, he would not be crucified; he would be institutionalized. A temperature of 98.6 is a fever to a race with spiritual hypothermia.

33

What is the historical significance of all the divisions and fragmentations that have emerged in the modern world since the end of the Middle Ages? And in modern households and families? And even in the forces of evil—materialism vs. "New Age" spiritualism, collectivism vs. individualism, Utopian optimistic humanism vs. nihilistic pessimism, etc.?

> MARK 3:24–26: "If a kingdom is divided against itself, that kingdom cannot stand. And if a house is divided against itself, that house will not be able to stand. And if Satan has risen up against himself and is divided, he cannot stand, but is coming to an end."

Evil is necessarily divisive and self-destructive. Why do we worry that the gates of Hell will prevail? We are seeing them fall apart.

34

Why is it that religious drug rehabilitation programs work so much more successfully and powerfully compared with merely ethical and humanistic and psychological ones, especially for the hardest cases? And why do A.A. and similar "twelve-step" programs that demand "reliance on a Higher Power" work, while other, secular ones do not? Why can't strong addictions usually be cured by psychology alone?

> MARK 3:27: "No one can enter a strong man's house and plunder his goods, unless he first binds the strong man; then indeed he may plunder his house."

(The identity of the "strong man" is revealed in verse 26.) The answer to the question is not psychological but cosmological. It is a problem of spiritual warfare. Only the Son of David can defeat the Father of Goliath.

35

Muhammad rejected Christ's claim to be the Son of God because he thought that "it is unfitting for God to have a son"—interpreting "son" physically. Nietzsche, on the other hand, understood Christ's claim (he had even attended a seminary) but rejected Christianity precisely because it stood for goodness, while Muhammad rejected it because he thought it was not *good. How will God judge these two rejections, one mental and one moral?*

> MARK 3:28–30: " 'Truly, I say to you, all sins will be forgiven the sons of men, and whatever blasphemies they utter; but whoever blasphemes against the Holy Spirit never has forgiveness, but is guilty of an eternal sin'—for they had said, 'He has an unclean spirit.' "

All God-seekers become God-finders, and none others do. All get what they want in the end. The great issue, then, is "what do you seek?" (Jn 1:38).

36

If I could be anyone in history, I would want to be Jesus' brother, cousin, or mother. Isn't it unfair that we do not know him as closely and intimately as his own family did?

> MARK 3:33–35: "And he replied, 'Who are my mother and my brethren?' And looking around on those who sat about him, he said, 'Here are my mother and my brethren! Whoever does the will of God is my brother, and sister, and mother.' "

Did Jesus have any sisters? That's up to you, sister!

37

What is the most important difference between people? What makes the biggest difference in the world? How are people best classified or differentiated?—Or is everybody the same?

Read MARK 4:2–20 (the parable of the sower). Same seed, separate soils.

The most valid way of classifying people is from God's point of view. What makes the biggest difference is what makes the *longest* difference: eternity.

In a story the villain may *think* he is as good as the hero, and a character who is destined to die may *think* he will live; but the Author's point of view is the only true one. And no author writes a story in which everybody is the same.

38

Why are there so few modern American saints? What is the most powerful practical obstacle to sanctity in modern American life?

> MARK 4:18: "And others are the ones sown among thorns; they are those who hear the word, but the cares of the world, and the delight in riches, and the desire for other things, enter in and choke the word, and it proves unfruitful."

Christianity's greatest apostle (Paul) went so far as to recommend avoiding God's greatest human invention (marriage) for this reason: see 1 Corinthians 7:32–33. Extreme solutions reflect extreme problems. But today, people *avoid* marriage because they love riches.

39

What is the purpose of education?

MARK 4:21: "Is a lamp brought in to be put under a bushel, or under a bed, and not on a stand?"

As food is for eating, truth is for teaching and learning. Hoarding knowledge from the ignorant is as wicked as hoarding food from the hungry. Truth is for teaching and teaching is for truth; as "food is meant for the stomach and the stomach for food" (1 Cor 6:13).

40

What is the point of the "Socratic method" of teaching, in which the teacher poses problems, puzzles, parables, and questions rather than just answers?

MARK 4:22: "For there is nothing hidden, except to be made manifest; nor is anything secret, except to come to light."

For the same reason, a striptease is more erotic than a nudist camp, and a puzzle solved is more interesting than an obvious truism.

41

What is the most effective method of learning?

MARK 4:23: "If any man has ears to hear, let him hear."

The essential thing in all learning, all education, all wisdom, is attention.

42

What is the secret of happiness? Why do some find this treasure and others do not?

> MARK 4:24: "The measure you give will be the measure you get."

There is no truth more plain, more practical, more wise, and more provable by daily experience than this one, yet also none more avoided.

43

Does Jesus teach any of the principles of capitalism?

> MARK 4:25: "To him who has will more be given; and from him who has not, even what he has will be taken away."

Therefore, invest boldly! It is *spiritual* capitalism, of course. Whether economic capitalism is good or not is another matter. But who really cares *passionately* about that?

44

What can we do to make sure people we love will believe? How does faith take root and grow in people?

MARK 4:26: "The kingdom of God is as if a man should scatter seed upon the ground, and should sleep and rise night and day, and the seed should sprout and grow, *he knows not how.* The earth produces of itself, first the blade, then the ear, then the full grain in the ear."

Another answer to the same question is Luke 11:5–13, which teaches patience *and* persistence in prayer. It's like farming.

45

Is progress a fact or a myth? Has there been any real progress in human history for the past two thousand years?

MARK 4:30–32: "With what can we compare the kingdom of God, or what parable shall we use for it? It is like a grain of mustard seed, which, when sown upon the ground, is the smallest of all the seeds on earth; yet when it is sown it grows up and becomes the greatest of all shrubs, and puts forth large branches, so that the birds of the air can make nests in its shade."

The answer is Yes, but only Heaven's newspaper reports earth's real headlines.

46

What are the cause and cure of fear?

MARK 4:40: "He said to them, 'Why are you afraid? Have you no faith?'"

Faith and fear are like heat and cold.

47

Has there ever been an infallible weather forecaster? If so, how?

MARK 4:41: "And they were filled with awe [after Jesus stilled the storm], and said to one another, 'Who then is this, that even wind and sea obey him?'"

The Author of the story has *authoritative* knowledge of the setting as well as the characters. *All* storms are raised *and* stilled by Him.

48

Goethe (in Faust*), Nietzsche (in* Beyond Good and Evil*), Hesse (in* Demian*), and many other modern writers justify and idealize experimenting with evil as a means to self-fulfillment and broadening one's personality. What fruit grows from the seed of this philosophy?*

MARK 5:2-9: "There met him out of the tombs a man with an unclean spirit, who lived among the tombs; and no one could bind him any more, even with a chain; for he had often been bound with shackles and chains, but the chains he wrenched apart, and the shackles he broke in pieces; and no one had the strength to subdue him. Night and day among the tombs and on the mountains he was always crying out, and bruising himself with stones. . . . And Jesus asked him, 'What is your name?' He replied, 'My name is Legion; for we are many.' "

Evil broadens your personality as dynamite "broadens" a building, or as a bullet to the head "broadens" your brains.

49

What can be done with your "dark side"? Is there a proper place for it?

MARK 5:11–13: "Now a great herd of swine was feeding there on the hillside; and they [the evil spirits] begged him, 'Send us to the swine, let us enter them.' So he gave them leave. And the unclean spirits came out, and entered the swine; and the herd, numbering about two thousand, rushed down the steep bank into the sea, and were drowned in the sea."

There is a universal gravitation. Everything seeks its proper place.

50

What would Jesus do for a nudist?

MARK 5:15: "And they came to Jesus, and saw the demoniac sitting there, clothed and in his right mind."

One Who is fully in His right mind can know what it is for us to be in our right mind and can restore us to it. We, who are not fully in our right mind, have not the right mind to know what *is* our right mind, much less restore ourselves to it, and its clothes.

51

What is the most convincing argument for Christianity?

> MARK 5:19–20: "[Jesus] said to him, 'Go home to your friends, and tell them how much the Lord has done for you, and how he has had mercy on you.' And he went away and began to proclaim in the Decapolis how much Jesus had done for him; and all men marveled."

There are always arguments against arguments; there are no arguments against experience.

52

If we saw Jesus truly, as He really is, what is the first thing we would do?

> MARK 5:22: "Then came one of the rulers of the synagogue, Jairus by name; and seeing him [Jesus], he fell at his feet."

See Revelation 1:17. Any other response means either that you do not know Him or that you do not know yourself.

53

How close do you have to get to Jesus for Him to "work"?

> MARK 5:27–29: "She had heard the reports about Jesus, and came up behind him in the crowd and touched his garment. For she said, 'If I touch even his garments, I shall be made well.' And immediately the hemorrhage ceased; and she felt in her body that she was healed of her disease."

The garment Jesus wears today is His Church on earth.

54

How do healing miracles work? Is it by the objective power of God or by the subjective power of belief? Is it God's power or my faith that heals me?

> MARK 5:30: "And Jesus, perceiving in himself that power had gone forth from him, immediately turned about in the crowd, and said, 'Who touched my garments?' "

> MARK 5:34: "And he said to her, 'Daughter, your faith has made you well.' "

The question is like asking whether sex takes place by the will of man or the will of woman. Or whether the bathtub is filled by the water (grace) or by opening the faucet (faith).

How should we face death, especially the death of a loved one?

MARK 5:35−36: "While he was still speaking, there came from the ruler's house some who said, 'Your daughter is dead. Why trouble the Teacher any further?' But ignoring what they said, Jesus said to the ruler of the synagogue, 'Do not fear, only believe.' "

Those people's saying was the only one Jesus ever found so stupid that He simply ignored it. It was like saying, "You're sick; don't trouble the doctor."

My friend has left the Church. She was baptized, and the seed of faith was planted in her when she was a baby; but it seems to have died out now. I feel exactly as if a beautiful little child—her faith—has died. Can anything be done?

MARK 5:39−42: "And when he had entered, he said to them, 'Why do you make a tumult and weep? The child is not dead but sleeping.' And they laughed at him. But he put them all outside, and took the child's father and mother and those who were with him, and went in where the child was. Taking her by the hand he said to her, 'Talitha cumi'; which means, 'Little girl, I say to you, arise.' And immediately the girl got up and walked."

The soil of the human heart has to be very cold for the seed of faith to die completely. Most times when we think it is dead, it is only dormant.

57

If God alone can raise the dead and save dead souls, what then remains for us to do, after telling this good news?

MARK 5:43: "And he . . . told them to give her something to eat."

The "daily bread" He asked us to pray for is not only symbolic. And it comes from Him through the hands and feet of His Body, us.

58

If Jesus—the same Jesus of the Gospels—came back to earth today, which church would He go to?

MARK 6:2: "And on the sabbath he began to teach in the synagogue."

A good Jew never abandons his people, even if most of them abandon him.

59

What is the most important question to ask about a preacher or evangelist?

MARK 6:2: "And many who heard him were astonished, saying, 'Where did this man get all this? What
is the wisdom given to him?'"

Successful theology is like successful politics: It's not
what you know, it's *Whom* you know.

60

*What one miracle did Muhammad perform that Jesus could
not?*

MARK 6:3–5: "'Is not this the carpenter, the son of
Mary and brother of James and Joses and Judas and
Simon, and are not his sisters here with us?' And
they took offense at him. And Jesus said to them,
'A prophet is not without honor, except in his own
country, and among his own kin, and in his own
house.' And he could do no mighty work there, except that he laid his hands upon a few sick people
and healed them."

Jesus performed many miracles. Muhammad performed
only one: his family (his wife) was his first disciple.

61

Everyone marveled at Jesus. What did Jesus marvel at?

MARK 6:6: "And he marveled because of their unbelief."

That is the one miracle a "dissenting" theologian can
perform.

For a successful missionary outreach, evangelism campaign, or church membership drive: (1) How many personnel are needed? (2) What is the major obstacle that must be overcome? (3) How much equipment and technology is needed? (4) How much funding is needed? (5) What media exposure or public platform should be secured? (6) How to avoid offending those who disagree?

MARK 6:7–11: "And he called to him the Twelve, and began to send them out [1] two by two, [2] and gave them authority over the unclean spirits. [3] He charged them to take nothing for their journey except a staff; no bread, no bag, [4] no money in their belts; but to wear sandals and not put on two tunics. [5] And he said to them, 'Where you enter a house, stay there until you leave the place. [6] And if any place will not receive you and they refuse to hear you, when you leave, shake off the dust that is on your feet for a testimony against them.' "

—And it worked!

What part of the Gospel (a) was the essential message of the apostles (b) as it was that of all the prophets, (c) is needed today more than ever before, and (d) is not preached but avoided today more than ever before?

MARK 6:12: "So they went out and preached that men should repent."

The Church of Pop Psychology is a non-prophet organization.

64

What did all Jesus' apostles do that 99 out of 100 preachers today do not do?

MARK 6:13: "And they cast out many demons."

Jesus came to fight a war.

65

If the architects of the "sexual revolution" found Aladdin's lamp, what would they ask the genie for?

> MARK 6:25: "I want you to give me at once the head of John the Baptist on a platter." (MARK 6:18–22: "For John said to Herod, 'It is not lawful for you to have your brother's wife.' And Herodias had a grudge against him, and wanted to kill him. . . . When Herodias' daughter came in and danced, she pleased Herod and his guests; and the king said to the girl, 'Ask me for whatever you wish, and I will grant it.'")

An addict eventually becomes a murderer. His addiction demands the death of anything that thwarts or threatens it. The empirical proof of this extreme-sounding proposition is the mutilated bodies of "unwanted" unborn babies in hospital dumpsters: victims of the slavish addiction to sexual "freedom".

Which directions that Jesus gave to his apostles are harder to obey the more technological "progress" we make? What was easier for Neanderthal man than for Jesus' apostles, easier for them than for our grandparents, and easier for our grandparents than for us?

MARK 6:31: "And he said to them, 'Come away by yourselves to a lonely place, and rest a while.'"

The more time-saving machines we invent, the less time we have.

What does Jesus think of the egalitarian modern world?

MARK 6:34: "As he landed he saw a great throng, and he had compassion on them, because they were like sheep without a shepherd."

In Jesus' authoritarian time, followers followed their leaders. In our egalitarian time, leaders follow their followers. Sheep without shepherds are still sheep.

What is the secret of finding time in a busy, busy world that seems to steal it all away? How can I multiply my hours?

MARK 6:41–44: "And taking the five loaves and the two fish he looked up to heaven, and blessed, and broke the loaves, and gave them to the disciples to set before the people; and he divided the two fish among them all. And they all ate and were satisfied. And they took up twelve baskets full of broken pieces and of the fish. And those who ate the loaves were five thousand men."

He does the same thing to our time, when we give it to Him, as He did to the loaves and fishes.

69

Why does God allow His children to be battered by a sea of troubles?

MARK 6:48: "And he saw that they were distressed in rowing, for the wind was against them. And about the fourth watch of the night he came to them, walking on the sea."

He wills the waves for the same reason a surfer does: He rides on them; He comes to us on them. And He knows that our true joy comes only from this: His coming to us, not from the absence of waves and troubles in our lives. Thus it is out of love that He raises waves.

70

When storms of troubles arise in our lives, what message are their winds breathing to us?

MARK 6:49–50: "But when they saw him walking on the sea they thought it was a ghost, and cried out;

for they all saw him, and were terrified. But immediately he spoke to them and said, 'Take heart, it is
I; have no fear.' "

The entire world echoes His words in the Eucharist:
"This is My Body." All sufferings say, "This is My
Blood" to the cells in His Mystical Body.

71

*My grandfather says his generation was much more moral
than ours because they avoided "uncleanliness". They believed that "cleanliness is next to godliness." He says the
most important thing is to hold onto "the good old days"
and "the good old ways". He expects his children to take
care of him, even though he never took care of his parents
when they were old because he gave all his money to religious
works. I wonder what God thinks of his philosophy?*

Read MARK 7:1–13.

Phariseeism is not confined to ancient Israel.

72

*Our church building is over one hundred years old. When
it was first built, the neighborhood was a beautiful suburb.
Now it is an inner-city ghetto. The church is moving out to
the suburbs because the congregation is afraid, not just of the
physical dangers, but of the spiritual. Right outside the church,
we see pimps and prostitutes and drug dealers and hear the
filthiest language you can imagine. We fear that this constant*

bombardment of evil that comes in through the eyes and ears will inevitably corrupt the soul. So we are moving out to the suburbs to save our souls, even though we feel uneasy about it because there are such terrible needs right here in the city. Are we doing the right thing and for the right reason?

Read MARK 7:14–23.

A doctor should not flee in fear from the diseases for which he claims to have the cure.

Matter cannot hurt spirit. You cannot punch a ghost. The soul can be harmed only from within. Jesus never fled from the evils without, only the evils within. Do you really think He would move to the suburbs?

73

What is the origin of evil?

> MARK 7:20: "And he said, 'What comes out of a man is what defiles a man. For from within, out of the heart of man, come evil thoughts, fornication, theft, murder, adultery, coveting, wickedness, deceit, licentiousness, envy, slander, pride, foolishness. All these evil things come from within, and they defile a man.'"

Look in the mirror to answer the question. Look with the I, not just the eye.

74

What did Socrates mean when he said that "no evil can happen to a good man, in this life or in the next"? He said that after he was unjustly found guilty of atheism and about to be executed. Very bad things were happening to this very good man; how could he deny this? Furthermore, he claimed to know nothing about the next life. How could he be sure his principle held true there, too?

> MARK 7:18–20: "And he said to them, 'Then are you also without understanding? Do you not see that whatever goes into a man from outside cannot defile him, since it enters, not his heart but his stomach, and so passes on? . . . What comes out of a man is what defiles a man.' "

The real dirt comes out the other end. Man differs from monkey in that his head is dirtier than his tail.

75

Our church has tried every trick to mount a publicity campaign, including PR men and TV time, but it is not working. Is there another way? How did Jesus become so famous?

> MARK 7:24: "And he entered a house, and would not have any one know it; yet he could not be hidden."

Goodness is humble, like water. But it also cannot be hidden, like light.

76

Animals test and play with each other's love on a physical level by pretending to rebuff or fight with each other. Human lovers sometimes play this game, too, on the romantic level, teasing each other. Did Jesus ever do this on the spiritual level?

Read MARK 7:24–30.

Why, if God is perfect love, does He not give us all the infinite fullness of eternal joy immediately and infallibly? Because perfect love does not force; it plays, patiently, with its beloved prey.

77

(1) I am terrified of public speaking. Can Jesus give me a talking tongue when I am shy and tongue-tied?

(2) I want to listen to the heart and will of God, but I am very poor at listening. Can Jesus give me the ears to hear Him?

> MARK 7:32–35: "And they brought to him a man who was deaf and had an impediment in his speech; and they begged him to lay his hand upon him. And taking him aside from the multitude privately, he put his fingers into his ears, and he spat and touched his tongue; and looking up to heaven, he sighed, and said to him, 'Ephphatha,' that is, 'Be opened.' And his ears were opened, his tongue was released, and he spoke plainly."

Whatever He heals in bodies, He heals in souls.

The modern world is a spiritual desert. How can we grow saints out of such sandy, secular soil? How can we find spiritual nourishment in such a nonspiritual environment?

MARK 8:4–5, 17–21: "And his disciples answered him, 'How can one feed these men with bread here in the desert?' And he asked them, 'How many loaves have you?' . . . Jesus said to them, 'Why do you discuss the fact that you have no bread? Do you not yet perceive or understand? Are your hearts hardened? Having eyes do you not see, and having ears do you not hear? And do you not remember? When I broke the five loaves for the five thousand, how many baskets full of broken pieces did you take up?'"

How much power is in one grain of sand? Enough to supply the whole world's energy needs for a century, if we had the nuclear technology. How much bread can the desert grow for us? Look at the miracle of agriculture in Israel today. How much spiritual potentiality is in the smallest soul? Enough for God to make out of it the greatest saint.

If God wants everyone to believe in Him, why does He not perform clear and undeniable miracles whenever we ask Him to? Why does He not walk into a science lab and invite us to perform all sorts of tests on Him?

MARK 8:11−12: "The Pharisees came and began to argue with him, seeking from him a sign from heaven, to test him. And he sighed deeply in his spirit, and said, 'Why does this generation seek a sign? Truly, I say to you, no sign shall be given to this generation.'"

Those who are determined not to believe do not need the signs and proofs they demand because they would not profit from them; and those determined to believe do not need them because they are already at the conclusion and do not need to go back to premises. If God proved His own existence with a perfect syllogism, skeptics would demand He prove His premises with yet another syllogism, et cetera ad infinitum. God did not give Moses proofs; He simply said, "I AM."

80

Why is the Church so worried about the theological heresies of Latin American "liberation theologians" when the primary problem there is not theology but hunger, just as those theologians say?

MARK 8:14−17: "Now they had forgotten to bring bread; and they had only one loaf with them in the boat. And he cautioned them, saying, 'Take heed, beware of the leaven of the Pharisees and the leaven of Herod.' And they discussed it with one another, saying, 'We have no bread.' And being aware of it, Jesus said to them, 'Why do you discuss the fact that you have no bread? Do you not yet perceive or understand?' "

The primary problem is always spiritual. The source of some people starving for bread is other people starving for moral wisdom.

81

Might myths be partial glimpses of Truth? To take one extreme example, could Tolkien's "ents"—walking, talking trees—possibly be an inspired work to heal and open our eyes, rather than mere fantasy, foolishness, folly, and falsehood to blind us?

> MARK 8:22–25: "And some people brought to him a blind man, and begged him to touch him. And he took the blind man by the hand, and led him out of the village; and when he had spit on his eyes and laid his hands upon him, he asked him, 'Do you see anything?' And he looked up and said, 'I see men; but they look like trees, walking.' Then again he laid his hands upon his eyes; and he looked intently and was restored, and saw everything clearly."

What prophets are to the moral will and philosophers to the mind, myths are to the imagination: providential preparations. What we see here through a glass, darkly, we will see in Heaven clearly, including the bits of Truth in the old tales.

*My "preachy" fundamentalist friend says, "Every Christian
is a witness, and every time is a time for preaching to your
unbelieving neighbor." I do not feel that way. Is he right? Is
he holier than I?*

> MARK 8:26: "And he [Jesus] sent him [the healed
> blind man] away to his home, saying, 'Do not even
> enter the village.' "

> MARK 8:30: "And he [Jesus] charged them [his apos-
> tles] to tell no one about him."

But see also Mark 8:38: "Whoever is ashamed of me
and of my words in this adulterous and sinful generation, of him will the Son of man also be ashamed,
when he comes in the glory of his Father with the
holy angels."

There is a time to speak and a time to be silent.

*I learned in a college theology course that there are many dif-
ferent theories about who Jesus was. Three of the most popular
are: (1) that He was a John the Baptist figure, a forerunner
of an even greater prophet to come. The greater prophet is
Muhammad, according to Muslims, or the "Maitreia", according to some new cults, or the Rev. Moon, according to the
Unification Church (the "Moonies"). (2) Hindus and Buddhists often say Jesus was a reincarnation of some previous*

*great prophet, like Moses or Elijah. (3) And humanists and
modernist theologians say He was just one of the prophets,
a good man—e.g., "the man-for-others"—but not divine.
How can I think my way through this confusing question?*

> MARK 8:27-29: "He asked his disciples, 'Who do
> men say that I am?' And they told him, [1] 'John the
> Baptist; and others say, [2] Elijah; and others [3] one
> of the prophets.' And he asked them, 'But who do
> you say that I am?' Peter answered him, 'You are
> the Christ.'"

The same old heresies are available in every age. So is
the simple truth.

84

What is the greatest theological mistake any pope ever made?

> MARK 8:31: "And he began to teach them that the
> Son of man must suffer many things, and be rejected
> by the elders and the chief priests and the scribes,
> and be killed, and after three days rise again. And
> he said this plainly. And Peter took him, and began
> to rebuke him. But turning and seeing his disciples,
> he rebuked Peter, and said, 'Get behind me, Satan!
> For you are not on the side of God, but of men.'"

Sometimes, "nuancing" the plain words of God is "re-
buking"—not just changing *interpretations*, but changing *sides*.

With which of the many different ways to self-realization taught by the many different schools of psychology would Jesus agree? How is the poor, fragile self to be saved?

MARK 8:34–35: "And he called to him the multitude with his disciples, and said to them, 'If any man would come after me, let him deny himself and take up his cross and follow me. For whoever would save his life will lose it; and whoever loses his life for my sake and the gospel's will save it.'"

Most modern psychology teaches you how to save yourself and lose your soul. Jesus teaches you how to lose yourself and save your soul.

Freud asks this question in Civilization and Its Discontents: *Modern man has become like a god, master of the forces of nature by his science and technology. Yet he is not happier than premodern man. Why? Freud thought the answer had something to do with sexual repression and guilt; but the Pill and the Sexual Revolution have pretty much removed the first, and Freudianism has removed the second, among major segments of the population—and yet they are not happy. Is there a simple, obvious psychological explanation for this?*

MARK 8:36: "For what does it profit a man, to gain the whole world and forfeit his life?" [KJV: lose his own soul?].

Ecclesiastes had everything, yet he had nothing. Job had nothing, yet he had everything.

87

Why do I need a Savior? Even if I have sold my soul to the Devil, like Faust, why can't I buy it back?

> MARK 8:37: "For what can a man give in return for his life?" [KJV: soul?].

Just as a camera can take a picture of anything in the world except its own insides, you can buy anything except yourself, the buyer. Besides, a life, a soul, is infinitely precious, so it demands an infinite price. Only God has that much capital.

88

What are we Christians supposed to say in a society where it is legal to display a Mapplethorpe photo of a man pissing into another man's mouth but not a Christmas manger scene in public; where the National Endowment for the Arts funds Serrano's "Piss Christ", a crucifix submerged in the "artist's" urine, but refuses to fund even first-rate "religious" art; where public schools dispense free condoms but forbid free prayers?

> MARK 8:38: "Whoever is ashamed of me and of my words in this adulterous and sinful generation, of him will the Son of man also be ashamed, when he

comes in the glory of his Father with the holy angels."

There are many things we may say to this, but silence
is certainly not one of them. Bonhoeffer said, "The
only thing that is necessary for the triumph of evil is
that the good do nothing." He wrote that from a Nazi
prison cell. The Greeks believed this law of Apollo:
"Nothing too much; moderation in all things." But
the true God said to the Laodicean church (Rev 3:16):
"Because you are lukewarm, and neither cold nor hot,
I will spew you out of my mouth."

89

When will God's kingdom come?

> MARK 9:1: "And he said to them, 'Truly, I say to
> you, there are some standing here who will not taste
> death before they see the kingdom of God come
> with power.'"

"You shall receive power when the Holy Spirit has
come upon you" (Acts 1:8). "Kingdom" means "reign".
"Reign" means "power". "The kingdom of God does
not consist in talk but in power" (1 Cor 4:20). What
power? Spiritual power. From where? From the Spirit.
When? Before death, not just after. Otherwise, it is
vain to pray "Thy kingdom come, thy will be done
on earth as it is in heaven."

If we could be totally objective, sober, realistic, and accurate, free from all subjective visions and illusions and fantasies, what would Jesus look like?

> MARK 9:2–3: "Jesus took with him Peter and James and John, and led them up a high mountain apart by themselves; and he was transfigured before them, and his garments became glistening, intensely white, as no fuller on earth could bleach them."

"Humankind cannot bear very much reality" (T. S. Eliot).

A. What empirical evidence is there that the dead still live?
B. What is the model for Jewish-Christian dialogue?

> MARK 9:4: "And there appeared to them Elijah with Moses; and they were talking to Jesus."

A. Christianity is much more like science than like philosophy or ideology: it is based on empirical evidence.

B. If the disciples of Moses and of Jesus imitate their teachers, they will dialogue with each other, too.

In the Holy Land, everywhere you go, there is a building, a church, or a shrine for every event in the Bible, it seems. Who

invented the idea of responding to holy events by buildings*?*
And what was in his head when he invented it?

> MARK 9:4–6: "And there appeared to them Elijah
> with Moses; and they were talking to Jesus. And
> Peter said to Jesus, 'Master, it is well that we are
> here; let us make three booths, one for you and one
> for Moses and one for Elijah.' For he did not know
> what to say."

A Gothic cathedral is not reasonable. It is a child's
awestruck, wordless "Oh!", responding to a glimpse
of Heaven, when we do not know what to say in
words.

93

*Who is the leading expert on Christology, and who does he
say Christ is?*

> MARK 9:7: "And a voice came out of the cloud,
> 'This is my beloved Son; listen to him.'"

There is a principle in scholarship: Primary sources
always take precedence over secondary sources. No-
where is this principle more reasonable and more necessary than in Christology.

94

*Hindus and Buddhists try to purify and unify and simplify
their consciousness, to free it from its usual multiplication and
distractions. What is the Christian version of this?*

MARK 9:8: "And suddenly looking around they no longer saw any one with them but Jesus only."

Less is sometimes more—as in makeup or in preaching (see 1 Cor 2:2).

95

Many theologians today "nuance" and "reinterpret" the plain and simple word of God. They seem to puzzle over the meaning of words that are perfectly plain to everyone else. When did this habit begin?

MARK 9:9–10: "And as they were coming down the mountain, he charged them to tell no one what they had seen, until the Son of man should have risen from the dead. So they kept the matter to themselves, questioning what the rising from the dead meant."

The thought that rising from the dead meant rising from the dead was too radical for them.

96

What does the world do to a prophet?

MARK 9:13: "But I tell you that Elijah has come, and they did to him whatever they pleased, as it is written of him."

A prophet does God's will to the world; the world does its own will to the prophet. Yet the prophet is fulfilled, and the world is frustrated.

What is the first and most immediate difference between people's attitude to Jesus two thousand years ago and people's attitude to Jesus today?

MARK 9:15: "And immediately all the crowd, when they saw him, were greatly amazed."

Jesus is Wisdom, true Wisdom.

Philosophy, true philosophy, is the love of wisdom.

Philosophy begins in wonder, according to its inventors, Socrates, Plato, Aristotle.

And wondering—questioning, questing—begins in amazement, not boredom.

What keeps us moderns most from Jesus is boredom.

Did Jesus ever complain?

MARK 9:19: "And he answered them, 'O faithless generation, how long am I to be with you? How long am I to bear with you?'"

See HEBREWS 4:15: "For we have not a high priest who is unable to sympathize with our weaknesses, but one who *in every respect* has been tempted as we are, yet without sinning."

The opposite of a nasty, self-centered complainer is not a nice, self-centered wimp. It is Christ, the complete Man.

99

What happens when Good and Evil meet?

> MARK 9:20: "And they brought the boy to him; and when the spirit saw him, immediately it convulsed the boy, and he fell on the ground and rolled about, foaming at the mouth."

The world foamed at the mouth when it saw Jesus. Especially on Good Friday. "Crucify Him!"—the thing we say again in every sin—those words come from Hell's mouth, foaming. Ever see a cornered rat?

100

Why is the world so bad? Does God lack the power *to heal it or the* compassion *to* want *to heal it? What's missing?*

> MARK 9:21–23: "And Jesus asked his father, 'How long has he had this?' And he said, 'From childhood. And it has often cast him into the fire and into the water, to destroy him; but if you can do anything, have pity on us and help us.' And Jesus said to him, 'If you can! All things are possible to him who believes.'"

The only thing that is missing to Him is our faith that nothing is missing to Him.

101

What things does faith make possible that are not possible without it?

MARK 9:23: "All things are possible to him who believes."

We are limited. If our faith *generated* possibilities, they would be limited. Since faith *receives* God's power, its possibilities are unlimited.

102

Suppose God were to ask me, "Are you a man of faith?" If I say Yes, I am self-righteous and proud. If I say No, I deny Him and the faith. What should I reply?

MARK 9:24: "Immediately the father of the child cried out and said, 'I believe; help my unbelief!'"

Only a believer ever says, "Lord, help my unbelief."

103

What's in a name? What power could words have in the real world?

MARK 9:25–26: "And when Jesus saw that a crowd came running together, he rebuked the unclean spirit, saying to it: 'You mute and deaf spirit, I command you, come out of him, and never enter him again.' And after crying out and convulsing him terribly, it came out."

The most powerful things last the longest, for everything seeks to preserve its own being, and power is first of all the power to do *that*. And "in the beginning was the Word, and the Word was with God, and the Word was God (Jn 1:1)." Therefore, there is nothing more powerful than the Word.

Jesus had power even over evil spirits. Why don't we have the same power? How can we get it?

> MARK 9:28–29: "And when he had entered the house, his disciples asked him privately, 'Why could we not cast it out?' And he said to them, 'This kind cannot be driven out by anything but prayer and fasting.'"

Prayer lets Jesus in. Jesus casts demons out. Demons keep prayer out.

What essential aspect of Christianity are we most unwilling to hear, unable to understand, and afraid to look into?

> MARK 9:30–32: "They went on from there and passed through Galilee. And he would not have any one know it; for he was teaching his disciples, saying to them, 'The Son of man will be delivered into the hands of men, and they will kill him; and when he is killed, after three days he will rise.' But they did not understand the saying, and they were afraid to ask him."

When did you last ask Him what in you had to die?

What is the underlying agenda of the chattering self?

MARK 9:33–34: "And they came to Capernaum; and when he was in the house he asked them, 'What were you discussing on the way?' But they were silent; for on the way they had discussed with one another who was the greatest."

Sports, war, debate, games, entrepreneurship, and clever party conversations all usually follow this agenda. Christ means to gavel that whole committee of chattering children away into oblivion.

Are all equal in Christ's kingdom?

MARK 9:35: "And he sat down and called the Twelve and he said to them, 'If any one would be first, he must be last of all and servant of all.' "

The Church is not a democracy. It is a Christocracy. Whoever is closest to His servanthood is closest to His lordship.

Give me one good reason for going through with an unplanned and unwanted pregnancy.

MARK 9:36–37 "And he took a child, and put him in the midst of them; and taking him in his arms, he said to them, 'Whoever receives one such child in my name receives me.'"

The One Who said, "Whatever you do to one of the least of my brothers, you do unto me" never lied and never exaggerated.

109

I understand 1 John 4:20: "If any one says, 'I love God,' and hates his brother, he is a liar; for he who does not love his brother whom he has seen, cannot love God whom he has not seen." But how can we love a God whom we have never seen? I can relate to and love and believe in Jesus. I know what and who Jesus was. I can imagine Jesus. But I cannot imagine God or see Him or even understand what an infinite, invisible, incomprehensible Being could be. How can I love one I have never seen?

MARK 9:37: "Whoever receives me, receives not me but him who sent me."

Christianity is not just for mystics and philosophers but is for humanists and empiricists. Although "no one has ever seen God" (Jn 1:18), yet "he who has seen me has seen the Father" (Jn 14:9).

110

What should we think of far-out fringe sects of Christians who set up shop far from main-line churches and do weird things like "casting out demons"?

MARK 9:38–39: "John said to him, 'Teacher, we saw a man casting out demons in your name, and we forbade him, because he was not following us.' But Jesus said, 'Do not forbid him; for no one who does a mighty work in my name will be able soon after to speak evil of me.'"

We should not be narrower than Jesus. (We should also not be broader than Jesus.)

III

Why is the Church so coldly negative? No adultery, no fornication, no divorce, no abortion, no contraception, no test-tube babies, no homosex, no surrogate motherhood, no transgenderism. Instead of warmth and approval, she dashes a cup of cold water on many human hopes and desires. In the name of what loveless philosophy does she do this? Won't she be punished for it in Heaven?

MARK 9:41: "Truly, I say to you, whoever gives you a cup of water to drink because you bear the name of Christ, will by no means lose his reward."

Love does not give warm water when the beloved needs cold. And isn't it remarkable that all of the world's complaints against the Church today concern her unchanging and unchangeable teachings about sexual morality? Are those the only "hopes and desires" today's world cares about?

What reward will the loving God give to liberal, tolerant, permissive teachers who free young people from old, terrible, burdensome philosophies of law and sin and guilt?

MARK 9:42: "Whoever causes one of these little ones who believe in me to sin, it would be better for him if a great millstone were hung round his neck and he were thrown into the sea."

The more you love children, the less you tolerate a bad pediatrician.

I say, if you have your health, you have everything. I have two good eyes, two good hands, and two good feet, and I would not exchange them for anything. Wouldn't Jesus say this is a wise philosophy?

MARK 9:43–48: "If your hand causes you to sin, cut it off; it is better for you to enter life maimed than with two hands to go to hell, to the unquenchable fire. And if your foot causes you to sin, cut it off; it is better for you to enter life lame than with two feet to be thrown into hell. And if your eye causes you to sin, pluck it out; it is better for you to enter the kingdom of God with one eye than with two eyes to be thrown into hell, where their worm does not die, and the fire is not quenched."

One who neglects his soul to care for his body is like one who dies in a fire trying to save his clothing.

114

The "Right", conservatives and traditionalists, say we should be proud to be distinctive, countercultural, and confrontational. The "Left", liberals and progressives, say we should seek peace. Who is right?

> MARK 9:50: "Salt is good; but if the salt has lost its saltiness, how will you season it? Have salt in yourselves, *and* be at peace with one another."

The Prince of Peace was also a salty character. He gives a different kind of peace from what the world gives: peace with God, self, and neighbor, not peace with the world, the flesh, and the Devil. He also gives a different kind of war from what the world gives: a war against principalities and powers, not flesh and blood.

115

Why won't the Church allow divorce?

> MARK 10:2, 9: " 'Is it lawful for a man to divorce his wife?' He answered them . . . 'What therefore God has joined together, let not man put asunder.' "

The Church refuses to allow divorce because she does not have the authority to correct Christ. Those who allow divorce claim more authority than she does.

There is conservative, traditional, absolutistic morality; and there is liberal, tolerant, permissive morality. Isn't the liberal morality more Christlike because it is rooted in compassion?

> MARK 10:2–5: "Pharisees . . . asked, 'Is it lawful for a man to divorce his wife?' He answered them, 'What did Moses command you?' They said, 'Moses allowed a man to write a certificate of divorce, and to put her away.' But Jesus said to them, 'For your *hardness of heart* he wrote you this commandment.' "

We let strangers, those we love less, and those we do not have high hopes for get away with evils and compromises. When our heart softens with love, we become more idealistic. Greater love means greater hope, greater expectations, and therefore greater intolerance of evil. That is why God put parents, not the State, in charge of children.

Isn't society the inventor of sexual identities?

> MARK 10:6: "But from the beginning of creation, 'God made them male and female.' "

Many people today use the word "Society" exactly where we always used to use the word "God". They even capitalize It.

If two people make a marriage, why can't they unmake it by divorce?

> MARK 10:9: "What . . . *God* has joined together, let not man put asunder."

It takes five people, not two, to make a marriage: a man, a woman, the Father, the Son, and the Holy Spirit. And three of them always vote against divorce.

Children, who invent the games they play, can change the rules any time they wish. But swimmers, who did not make the sea, must swim by its laws once they dive in.

If the Church's "no divorce" philosophy were true, there would be an absurd consequence: every time a divorced man had sex with his second wife, he would be committing adultery against his first wife, even though they were divorced. Where did the Church ever get such an absurd idea in the first place?

> MARK 10:10–12: "And in the house the disciples asked him again about this matter. And he said to them, 'Whoever divorces his wife and marries another, commits adultery against her; and if she divorces her husband and marries another, she commits adultery.'"

No one can read the Bible for long without coming to a place where he must choose either to correct God's mind or to let God correct his.

120

Jesus often got angry at the Pharisees. Did he ever get angry at his own disciples?

MARK 10:13–14: "And they were bringing children to him, that he might touch them; and the disciples rebuked them. But when Jesus saw it he was indignant, and said to them, 'Let the children come to me, do not hinder them; for to such belongs the kingdom of God.'"

Love is always indignant when the powerful harm the powerless. That is why gentle Jesus is angry at abortion.

121

What is adult Christianity?

MARK 10:15: "Truly, I say to you, whoever does not receive the kingdom of God like a child shall not enter it."

"Adult Christianity"—now what could that mean? Think of what the word "adult" means in our culture. What are "adult" movies, "adult" bookstores? Jesus' Christianity is unadulterated.

What is the most intelligent question ever asked?

MARK 10:17: "A man ran up and knelt before him, and asked him, 'Good Teacher, what must I do to inherit eternal life?'"

How is it that many of the most intelligent scholars, philosophers, scientists, and writers do not ask this question?

Why do bad things happen to good people?

MARK 10:18: "No one is good but God alone."

An unanswerable question is usually hiding a false assumption.

If we keep the Ten Commandments, will we go to Heaven?

MARK 10:20: "And he said to him, 'Teacher, all these [commandments] I have observed from my youth.' And Jesus looking upon him loved him, and said to him, 'You lack one thing . . . follow me.'"

The entrance ticket to Heaven is not a good grade on the Commandment Test. For one thing, that report card is not in our pocket. For another thing, even if it were in our pocket, it would be in *our* pocket. The ticket is Jesus. He does not fit into our pockets.

I am very rich and very practical. I do not suppose that Jesus, who was neither, has any advice in which I would be interested. I am looking for an investment counselor to find me the most practical possible use for my money. Isn't Jesus totally irrelevant to that?

> MARK 10:21: "Go, sell what you have, and give to the poor, and you will have treasure in heaven; and come, follow me."

Jesus was the most practical person who ever lived.

126

What is the most dangerous thing in the world?

> MARK 10:23: And Jesus looked around and said to his disciples, 'How hard it will be for those who have riches to enter the kingdom of God!' "

We all touch one of the most dangerous things in the world every day. It is to the soul what flypaper is to a fly.

127

Jesus' disciples were utterly astounded at two of His sayings. One of them was His prediction of His death and His insistence that He had come to suffer and die. This idea is by now familiar and largely accepted among Christians. Not so with the second; we are as startled and incredulous at it as the apostles were. What idea is this?

MARK 10:23–26: "And Jesus looked around and said to his disciples, 'How hard it will be for those who have riches to enter the kingdom of God!' And the disciples were amazed at his words."

Christ's social morality scandalizes the Right as much as His sexual morality scandalizes the Left because the Left treats sex like money—a commodity for exchange —while the Right treats money like sex—make love to it, and make it pregnant.

128

What is harder than putting the toothpaste back into the tube?

MARK 10:25: "It is easier for a camel to go through the eye of a needle than for a rich man to enter the kingdom of God."

The price of admission to Heaven is total poverty. You can't take anything with you.

129

Dostoyevsky said, "All things are permissible without God." What happens with *God?*

MARK 10:27: "All things are possible with God."

Without God, everything is permissible, but not everything is possible. With God, not everything is permissible, but everything is possible.

As a gambler, I look for three-to-one odds or better. So what must I be prepared to give up, and what three things will I gain, if I follow Christ?

> MARK 10:29–30: "Jesus said, 'Truly, I say to you, there is no one who has left house or brothers or sisters or mother or father or children or lands, for my sake and for the gospel, who will not receive [1] a hundredfold now in this time, houses and brothers and sisters and mothers and children and lands, [2] with persecutions, [3] and in the age to come eternal life.' "

Jesus is the only employer with 100 percent honest advertising.

I asked a wise old Christian, "Who do you think were the ten greatest persons who ever lived?", and I don't understand the reply, "I don't think you would recognize most of the names." What did this mean?

> MARK 10:31: "Many that are first will be last, and the last first."

In a good drama, the audience is surprised at how the characters turn out, but the author is not. In Heaven, we will all have surprises except God.

Why doesn't the whole world follow Jesus? What are they afraid of?

> MARK 10:32–34: "And they were on the road, go-
> ing up to Jerusalem, and Jesus was walking *ahead*
> of them; and they were *amazed*, and those who fol-
> lowed were *afraid*. And taking the Twelve again, he
> began to tell them what was to happen to him, say-
> ing, 'Behold, we are going up to Jerusalem; and the
> Son of man will be delivered to the chief priests and
> the scribes, and they will condemn him to death,
> and deliver him to the Gentiles; and they will mock
> him, and spit upon him, and scourge him, and kill
> him; and after three days he will rise.' "

The real Jesus walks *ahead* of us, His disciples are
amazed, and those at a distance are *afraid*. The Jesus
the world prefers walks *behind* us, in our steps, instead
of us in His; His disciples are *bored*, and those at a distance are *comforted*.

Teach us how not *to pray.*

> MARK 10:35: "And James and John, the sons of
> Zebedee, came forward to him, and said to him,
> 'Teacher, we want you to do for us whatever we
> ask of you.' "

By nature, we want *God* to say to *us*, "Hallowed be *thy* name; *thy* kingdom come; *thy* will be done." By nature, we are spiritually insane.

134

What are those individuals or groups who are asking for "empowerment" in the Church really asking for?

> MARK 10:37–39: "And they said to him, 'Grant us to sit, one at your right hand and one at your left, in your glory.' But Jesus said to them, 'You do not know what you are asking. Are you able to drink the chalice that I drink, or to be baptized with the baptism with which I am baptized?' And they said to him, 'We are able.' And Jesus said to them, 'The chalice that I drink you will drink; and with the baptism with which I am baptized, you will be baptized.'"

In His kingdom, power means martyrdom. Those who ask for "empowerment" in the Church have a different kingdom in mind, and a different king.

135

Did Jesus teach any distinctive new social and political philosophy?

> MARK 10:42–45: "And Jesus called them to him and said to them, 'You know that those who are supposed to rule over the Gentiles lord it over them,

and their great men exercise authority over them. But it shall not be so among you; but whoever would be great among you must be your servant, and whoever would be first among you must be slave of all. For the Son of man also came not to be served but to serve, and to give his life as a ransom for many.' "

There are three philosophies of social structure: (1) hierarchy, superiority, and authority; (2) equality; and (3) Christianity. Premodern Christians usually confused (3) with (1); modern Christians usually confuse (3) with (2).

136

The Incarnation seems like a military invasion: God entering enemy-occupied territory, in disguise, to win back His children from the Devil, who captured them back in the Garden of Eden. But the operation seems like a failure. For only a few people believed and served Him. Most refused. In fact, most of them screamed for His blood—"Crucify him!"— and they got it. Any military occupation that fails to accomplish its purpose is a failure. Why wasn't the Incarnation a failure?

> MARK 10:45: "For the Son of man also came not to be served but to serve, and to give his life as a ransom for many."

They screamed for His blood, and they got it. That is why He came: to donate blood. He succeeded.

If I am not blind to who I am and to who Jesus is, I am enlightened. What would an enlightened person say to Jesus if he knew He was passing through his hometown?

MARK 10:46–47: "And they came to Jericho; and as he was leaving Jericho with his disciples and a great multitude, Bartimaeus, a blind beggar, the son of Timaeus, was sitting by the roadside. And when he heard that it was Jesus of Nazareth, he began to cry out and say, 'Jesus, Son of David, have mercy on me!' "

This "blind" man saw more clearly than the sighted.

If reincarnation were true, of whom would the Supreme Court judges who banned prayer in public schools be reincarnations?

MARK 10:47–48: "And when he [blind Bartimaeus] heard that it was Jesus of Nazareth, he began to cry out and say, 'Jesus, Son of David, have mercy on me!' And many rebuked him, telling him to be silent."

Prayer is "offensive"; obscenity is "free expression".

What is the practical and reasonable thing to do when you are the victim of religious censorship?

MARK 10:48: "And many rebuked him, telling him to be silent; but he cried out all the more, 'Son of David, have mercy on me!' "

And it worked! It still does.

140

What is our only hope, both in this life and in the next?

MARK 10:49: "And Jesus stopped and said, 'Call him.' And they called the blind man, saying to him, 'Take heart; rise, *he is calling you.*' "

That is why you were born. That is why you will go to Heaven. And that is why you pray.

141

How should we respond to God's call?

MARK 10:50: "And [1] throwing off his cloak he [2] sprang up and [3] came to Jesus."

(1) HEBREWS 12:1: "Therefore, since we are surrounded by so great a cloud of witnesses, let us also lay aside every weight, and sin which clings so closely . . ."

(2) ROMANS 13:11: "You know what hour it is, how it is full time now for you to wake from sleep. For salvation is nearer to us now. . . ."

(3) MATTHEW 11:28: "Come to me, all who labor and are heavy laden, and I will give you rest."

What is the first thing for which we would ask God if we were truly wise?

> MARK 10:51: "And Jesus said to him, 'What do you want me to do for you?' And the blind man said to him, 'Master, let me receive my sight.'"

Solomon (1 Kings 3) showed wisdom in asking God for wisdom. The first thing to ask for is the wisdom to know what second things to ask for.

Many philosophers say reason is superior to faith because reason provides certainty, through proof, which faith does not. Can faith do anything that reason cannot do?

> MARK 10:52: "And Jesus said to him, 'Go your way; your faith has made you well.' And immediately he received his sight and followed him on the way."

Reason is like a medical library. Faith is like consent to an operation.

How inalienable is our right to private property?

> MARK 11:1–3: "And when they drew near to Jerusalem, to Bethphage and Bethany, at the Mount of Olives, he sent two of his disciples, and said to them, 'Go into the village opposite you, and

immediately as you enter it you will find a colt tied, on which no one has ever sat; untie it and bring it. If any one says to you, "Why are you doing this?" say, "The Lord has need of it and will send it back here immediately." ' "

Our rights yield to His needs. Yet He also respects and returns our rights. He still has needs, for He still has a Body here on earth.

145

Does Jesus want regality or simplicity? Is He grand or humble? On a high horse or on our level?

MARK 11:7–10: "And they brought the colt to Jesus, and threw their garments on it; and he sat upon it. And many spread their garments on the road, and others spread leafy branches which they had cut from the fields. And those who went before and those who followed cried out, 'Hosanna! Blessed is he who comes in the name of the Lord! Blessed is the kingdom of our father David that is coming! Hosanna in the highest!' "

It is the humblest One who deserves the highest hosannas.

146

What happens to those whose faith bears no fruit of good works?

MARK 11:12–14: "On the following day, when they came from Bethany, he was hungry. And seeing in

76

the distance a fig tree in leaf, he went to see if he could find anything on it. When he came to it, he found nothing but leaves, for it was not the season for figs. And he said to it, 'May no one ever eat fruit from you again.'"

He answered that question: "Every branch of mine that bears no fruit, he takes away" (Jn 15:2). "Faith apart from works is barren" (Jas 2:20).

147

Was the Prince of Peace a pacifist?

MARK 11:15-16: "And they came to Jerusalem. And he entered the temple and began to drive out those who sold and those who bought in the temple, and he overturned the tables of the money-changers and the seats of those who sold pigeons; and he would not allow any one to carry anything through the temple."

Unrighteous anger is sin, but lack of righteous anger at what deserves it is also sin. Jesus was without sin. Therefore He was not without righteous anger.

148

What does Jesus say about rich televangelists?

MARK 11:17: "And he taught, and said to them, 'Is it not written, "My house shall be called a house of

prayer for all the nations"? But you have made it a
den of robbers.' "

"The only good argument against Christianity is [some]
Christians" (Chesterton).

What scares scholars most?

> MARK 11:18: "The scribes heard it and sought a way
> to destroy him; for they feared him, because all the
> multitude was astonished at his teaching."

Children are the first to be astonished. Scribes and
scholars are the exorcists of astonishment.

*Why are we surprised when divine punishments that were
threatened to apostate individuals or nations materialize?*

> MARK 11:20–22: "As they passed by in the morning,
> they saw the fig tree withered away to its roots. And
> Peter remembered and said to him, 'Master, look!
> The fig tree which you cursed has withered.' And
> Jesus answered them, 'Have faith in God.' "

If our faith were full, our fear *and* our love would be
full, too.

If you have faith in God, you believe His punishments as well as His rewards.

151

Scientists tell us that we use only one-tenth of our brains and that there is enough untapped nuclear energy in a pea to destroy a planet. How much of the power of faith does the greatest saint release?

> MARK 11:23: "Truly, I say to you, whoever says to this mountain, 'Be taken up and cast into the sea,' and does not doubt in his heart, but believes that what he says will come to pass, it will be done for him."

Jesus also said (Mt 17:20), "Truly, I say to you, if you have faith as a grain of mustard seed, you will say to this mountain, 'Move from here to there,' and it will move." Since we have not seen any mountains moving, we can conclude that we have not seen any faith quite as big as a grain of mustard seed.

152

Is there any sin God can't forgive?

> MARK 11:25: "And whenever you stand praying, forgive, if you have anything against any one; so that your Father also who is in heaven may forgive you your trespasses."

God forgives every sin. But if the hands of your soul are not open to give forgiveness, they cannot be open to receive it, either. Therefore, unforgivingness is the unforgivable sin.

153

What dialogue would take place if Jesus returned today and walked into the editorial office of the New York Times*?*

MARK 11:27-33 (with minor updating changes): "And they came again to New York. And as he was walking into the *Times* building, the chief priests and the scribes and the elders of that church came to him, and they said to him, 'By what authority are your bishops saying these things, or who gave them the authority to say them?' Jesus said to them, 'I will ask you a question; answer me, and I will tell you by what authority they say these things. Were the Ten Commandments from heaven or from men? Answer me.' And they argued with one another, 'If we say, "from heaven," he will say, "Why then do you not believe them?" But shall we say "From men"?'—they were afraid of the people, for all held that Moses was a prophet. So they answered, 'We do not know.' And Jesus said to them, 'Neither will I tell you by what authority my bishops say these things.'"

An insincere question should first be required to prove its right to an answer before it is answered.

154

What is the most effective way to deliver a needed message that your hearers would like to ignore and forget?

MARK 12:1: "And he began to speak to them in para-bles."

Stories are like music: unlike abstract ideas, they slip into the soul's unconscious, past the censors at con-sciousness' gate.

155

Summarize the history of the world from God's point of view. What is His business?

Read MARK 12:1-9 (the parable of the vineyard).

God is in the farming business and the wine-making business.

156

How does a God of love deal with apostates?

MARK 12:9: "What will the owner of the vineyard do? He will come and destroy the [apostate] ten-ants, and give the vineyard to others."

God's love, like the sun, shines on the just and the un-just. But the unjust pull down the shades, so the light gives itself to the just, instead. He will do the same thing to Christians that He did to the Jews: when most of Israel rejected Him, He moved His vineyard (His Church) to Europe (the West). Now that the West has also rejected Him, He is turning to the "Third World".

How can you reconcile the belief that the Jews are God's "chosen people" with the fact that most Jews, and official Judaism, rejected Jesus as the Messiah and continue to do so?

> MARK 12:10–11: "Have you not read this Scripture: 'The very stone which the builders rejected has become the cornerstone; this was the Lord's doing, and it is marvelous in our eyes'?"

A "reasonable" God would have chosen the Egyptians or the Greeks or the Romans. A "reasonable" Christ would have come to Greece with philosophy or to Rome with power, and been lionized. But the God of Abraham is "the Lord of the absurd". See 1 Corinthians 1:18–29.

Kant said, "Two things fill my soul with wonder: the starry sky above and the moral law within." Why do we find these two things wonderful?

> MARK 12:11: "This was the Lord's doing, and [therefore] it is marvelous in our eyes."

Wonder always perceives the presence of God, however dimly.

How can you get away with publicly criticizing a dictator?

MARK 12:12: "And they tried to arrest him, *but feared the multitude*, for they perceived that he had told the parable against them; so they left him and went away."

The masters always fear their slaves.

Was Jesus ever interviewed on a talk show?

MARK 12:13: "And they sent to him some of the Pharisees and some of the Herodians, to entrap him in his talk."

And He handled His "handlers" so well that they did not try it again until twenty centuries later.

What would Jesus say to Americans who make a religion of politics and politicize their religion?

MARK 12:17: "Render to Caesar the things that are Caesar's, and to God the things that are God's."

That is what God says. Now, if Caesar would only say the same thing . . .

Could you imagine Jesus as an IRS agent?

> MARK 12:15–17: " 'Bring me a coin, and let me look at it.' And they brought one. And he said to them, 'Whose likeness and inscription is this?' They said to him, 'Caesar's.' Jesus said to them, 'Render to Caesar the things that are Caesar's.' "

In becoming a man, He made all men holy. In becoming a carpenter, He made all legitimate jobs holy, even that of the tax collector.

163

If you marry Mister or Miss Right, is he or she yours forever? If you marry Mister or Miss Wrong, are you stuck with him or her for eternity?

> MARK 12:25: "When they rise from the dead, they neither marry nor are given in marriage."

Eternal weights are not put on temporal shoulders.

164

What word did Jesus always pronounce wrong?

> MARK 12:18, 24: "And Sadducees came to him, who say that there is no resurrection. . . . Jesus said to them, '. . . you are wrong.' "

The word is "wrong".

Where do most theological errors come from?

> MARK 12:24: "Jesus said to them, 'Is not this why you are wrong, that you know neither the Scriptures nor the power of God?'"

Many theologians know the Scriptures only as Albert Einstein knew his math, not as he knew his wife.

166

When I die, people on earth will eventually forget me, but God will remember me forever, won't He?

> MARK 12:26–27: "And as for the dead being raised, have you not read in the book of Moses, in the passage about the bush, how God said to him, 'I *am* the God of Abraham, and the God of Isaac, and the God of Jacob'? He is not God of the dead, but of the living.'"
>
> Luke adds: "for all live to him" (Lk 20:38).

We keep the past "alive" in our memories. God has no need of memory because He has no past; He makes everything present, including all of us, even our past.

167

Walker Percy describes one of his characters as getting A's in all his subjects but flunking life. How do you avoid this fate?

> MARK 12:28: "And one of the scribes came up and heard them disputing with one another, and seeing that he answered them well, asked him, "Which commandment is the first of all?" "

Not to ask for "the one thing necessary" is not to get it. The Big Answer comes only to the Big Question, as the big lollipop fits only into a big mouth.

168

Everyone defines love as a feeling. Is it?

> MARK 12:28-31: " 'Which commandment is the first of all?' Jesus answered, 'The first is, "Hear, O Israel: The Lord our God, the Lord is one; and you shall love the Lord your God with all your heart, and with all your soul, and with all your mind, and with all your strength." The second is this, "You shall love your neighbor as yourself." ' "

Feelings cannot be commanded. Commanding what cannot be commanded is self-contradictory. A wise teacher does not teach what is self-contradictory. Jesus is a wise teacher. Therefore, love is not a feeling.

169

Is it not unrealistic and simplistic to be fanatical and absolutely single-minded about anything?

> MARK 12:32-34: "And the scribe said to him, 'You are right, Teacher; you have truly said that he is

one, and there is no other but he; and to love him with all the heart, and with all the understanding, and with all the strength, and to love one's neighbor as oneself, is much more than all whole burnt offerings and sacrifices.' And when Jesus saw that he answered wisely, he said to him, 'You are not far from the kingdom of God.' And after that no one dared to ask him any question."

"Fanatic" is modernity's F-word. But every real lover is a fanatic ("with *all* the heart, and with *all* the understanding, and with *all* the strength"). Therefore, love is really modernity's F-word.

170

How did Jesus reconcile apparently contradictory passages of Scripture about Himself?

MARK 12:35–37: "And as Jesus taught in the temple, he said, 'How can the scribes say that the Christ is the son of David? David himself, inspired by the Holy Spirit, declared, "The Lord said to my Lord, Sit at my right hand, till I put your enemies under your feet." David himself calls him Lord; so how is he his son?' "

The answer to the Speaker's puzzle is the Speaker Himself. The Word of God is one and not many, not contradictory, because it is a "He", not an "it". This Book is a portrait; each word is a molecule in His face.

What talk would Jesus give at a theologians' conference?

MARK 12:38: "Beware of the scribes."

This scribe had better not inscribe a commentary on that!

What criminals receive the worst punishments in Hell?

MARK 12:38: "Beware of the scribes, who like to go about in long robes, and to have salutations in the market places and the best seats in the synagogues and the places of honor at feasts, who devour widows' houses and for a pretense make long prayers. They will receive the greater condemnation."

Heaven and Hell are not in all ways opposite to each other. In one way, they are *both* opposite to earth and similar to each other: on earth, truth is hidden, and appearance and reality do not coincide, and justice is not done; while in both Heaven and Hell, everyone appears as he is, and truth and justice are done. That is why many of the temporally first will be eternally last, and the temporally last will be eternally first.

Aristotle taught that wealth was desirable because it makes possible the virtue of magnanimity, or grandiose generosity, since you can be more generous when you have more to give; you can not only do more good but also be more virtuous when

you have more financial wherewithal with which to do good.
Is this true?

> MARK 12:41–44: "And he sat down opposite the
> treasury, and watched the multitude putting money
> into the treasury. Many rich people put in large
> sums. And a poor widow came, and put in two cop-
> per coins, which make a penny. And he called his
> disciples to him, and said to them, 'Truly, I say to
> you, this poor widow has put in more than all those
> who are contributing to the treasury. For they all
> contributed out of their abundance; but she out of
> her poverty has put in everything she had, her whole
> living.'"

The measure of your generosity is not how much you
give but how much you keep. In fact, the poor are
usually more generous than the rich.

174

What does Jesus think of Western civilization?

> MARK 13:1–2: "And as he came out of the temple,
> one of his disciples said to him, 'Look, Teacher,
> what wonderful stones and what wonderful build-
> ings!' And Jesus said to him, 'Do you see these great
> buildings? There will not be left here one stone
> upon another, that will not be thrown down.'"

Our civilization, like most of the individuals in it, does
not face its one supremely certain fact: its own mor-
tality.

Are there any concrete clues to the mystery of how near we are to the end of the world?

MARK 13:4–12: "When will this be, and what will be the sign when these things are all to be accomplished?"

(A) "Many will come in my name, saying, 'I am he!' And they will lead many astray."

(B) "And when you hear of wars and rumors of wars, do not be alarmed; this must take place, but the end is not yet. For nation will rise against nation, and kingdom against kingdom; there will be earthquakes in various places, there will be famines; this is but the beginning of the sufferings."

(C) "And the gospel must first be preached to all nations."

(D) "And brother will deliver up brother to death, and the father his child, and children will rise against parents."

Mothers slaughtering their own unborn children is an even more apocalyptic sign.

What is the job description for a missionary?

MARK 13:9, 13: "They will deliver you up to councils; and you will be beaten in synagogues; and you will stand before governors and kings for my sake, to bear testimony before them . . . and you will be hated by all for my name's sake."

All applicants for this job are either naïve, insane, or in love.

177

How did the apostles move people with their sermons? How did Peter change the hearts of three thousand people with one sermon (Acts 2:14–41)? How did Paul nearly convert a king (Agrippa, Acts 26)? The sermons we hear Sunday after Sunday seem dull and unmoving; yet their preachers have the advantage of two thousand years of theology and years of seminary training. How did the apostles do it?

> MARK 13:11: "And when they bring you to trial and deliver you up, do not be anxious beforehand about what you are to say; but say whatever is given you in that hour, for it is not you who speak, but the Holy Spirit."

What would produce great sermons again? Persecutions plus Pentecost.

178

Modernity may be a spiritual regress, but at least it has made great physical progress, especially in relieving human suffering. Can we reasonably look forward to continual progress in this area?

> MARK 13:19: "For in those [last] days there will be such tribulation as has not been from the beginning of the creation which God created until now."

Walker Percy says that "compassion led to the gas chambers." I think he meant that the worship of freedom from suffering as the highest good eventually results in maximum suffering. To explain this paradox, read *A Canticle for Leibowitz* by Walter M. Miller, Jr., C. S. Lewis' favorite science fiction novel and mine, too.

179

Could the powers of evil ever become so strong in this world that eventually the whole world would be nothing but one vast breeding ground for Hell, and no one in the whole world would be saved?

> MARK 13:20: "And if the Lord had not shortened the days, no human being would be saved; but for the sake of the elect, whom he chose, he shortened the days."

Not only *can* this be, it *will* be, unless Christ was a false prophet. The road to Hell is paved with signs of "Progress". As the damned fall into the flames, they chant "Onward and upward!" .

180

Couldn't the Rev. Moon (of the "Moonies") be Jesus Christ come back again, as he claimed?

> MARK 13:21: "If any one says to you, 'Look, here is the Christ!' or 'Look, there he is!' do not believe it."

Only a fool mistakes the Moon for the Son.

Who but God or someone empowered by God could perform apparent miracles?

> MARK 13:22: "False Christs and false prophets will arise and show signs and wonders, to lead astray, if possible, the elect."

"God is not in strength but in truth" (Gandhi).

Can we rely on the order of nature? Will the cosmic order last for billions of years after the human race becomes extinct on this planet, just as it existed for billions of years before we appeared on this planet?

> MARK 13:24-25: "But in those days, after that tribulation, the sun will be darkened, and the moon will not give its light, and the stars will be falling from heaven, and the powers in the heavens will be shaken."

When it is time for the actors to exit, the play is over and the scenery is removed, too.

Is the doctrine of the divinity of Christ purely a matter of faith, or is it empirically testable? Is it not meaningless from a scientific point of view, since it is not in any way visible?

MARK 13:26: "And then they will see the Son of man coming in clouds with great power and glory."

History is a laboratory. Faith is an experiment. The definitive result will soon be in.

184

How will those who are alive at the end of the world get to Heaven? What will be their mode of transportation?

MARK 13:27: "And then he will send out the angels, and gather his elect from the four winds, from the ends of the earth to the ends of heaven."

The real Trans-World Airlines has a fleet of angels.

185

Is it not silly for some preachers to claim to see evidence that we are near the end of the world?

MARK 13:28–29: "From the fig tree learn its lesson: as soon as its branch becomes tender and puts forth its leaves, you know that summer is near. So also, when you see these things taking place, you know that he is near, at the very gates."

When a detective finds clues, he would be just as foolish to ignore them as to dogmatize about them.

Less than forty years after Jesus' death, there came the death of Old Testament Judaism, the temple, and the holy city of Jerusalem, in A.D. 70. Who ever predicted that?

> MARK 13:30: "Truly, I say to you, this generation will not pass away before all these things take place."

History's trains always obey prophecy's timetables.

We know everything is changing today. Everything once thought to be solid, safe, and stable is loosening up, from Newtonian physics to marriage and the family. The very stars, which the ancients fondly thought to be eternal, we know to be vast, dynamic processes of birth, growth, decay, and death. Is there anything we can see and know in this world that is unchangeable? The world itself is dying; can anything in it be undying?

> MARK 13:31: "Heaven and earth will pass away, but my words will not pass away."

Before the Word was in the world, the world was in the Word (Jn 1:1). Our words are like pyramids: the longest-lasting of them eventually crumble. His words are like the principles of geometry: uncrumbleable.

On what subject do thousands of Christians claim to know more than Christ and the angels?

> MARK 13:32: "But of that day or that hour [the end of the world] no one knows, not even the angels in heaven, nor the Son, but only the Father."

Even Christ could say "I don't know." Why do some Christians find those words so unpronounceable?

What difference does this "far-out" doctrine of the Second Coming of Christ at the end of the world make to me and Monday morning? Is it not a distraction?

> MARK 13:34–37: "It is like a man going on a journey, when he leaves home and puts his servants in charge, each with his work, and commands the doorkeeper to be on the watch. Watch therefore —for you do not know when the master of the house will come, in the evening, or at midnight, or at cockcrow, or in the morning—lest he come suddenly and find you asleep."

That is a good part of the reason why the Church seems sleepy today compared with the early Church, which seemed so alive and awake.

Wouldn't Jesus have thought it foolish and immoral of the Middle Ages to build enormous, and enormously expensive, Gothic cathedrals while most of the people were living in poverty?

> MARK 14:3–6: "And while he was at Bethany in the house of Simon the leper, as he sat at table, a woman came with an alabaster jar of ointment of pure nard, very costly, and she broke the jar and poured it over his head. But there were some who said to themselves indignantly, 'Why was the ointment thus wasted? For this ointment might have been sold for more than three hundred denarii, and given to the poor.' And they reproached her. But Jesus said, 'Let her alone; why do you trouble her? She has done a beautiful thing to me.'"

See John 12:4 for the identity of this objector, the patron saint of self-righteously cheap Christians.

Who was the first Christian to accept a government grant?

> MARK 14:10–11: "Then Judas Iscariot, who was one of the Twelve, went to the chief priests in order to betray him to them. And when they heard it they were glad, and promised to give him money."

Many Christians, like Judas, spend more time and passion thinking about money than about Jesus. Do you?

Light and water were the first two things created (Gen 1:3–8). They are universally used as symbols for Truth and Life. Three wise men followed light (a star) to Jesus' birth. Who followed water to prepare for His death?

> MARK 14:12–13: "And on the first day of Unleavened Bread, when they sacrificed the Passover lamb, his disciples said to him, 'Where will you have us go and prepare for you to eat the Passover?' And he sent two of his disciples, and said to them, 'Go into the city, and a man carrying a jar of water will meet you; follow him.'"

We, too, can follow water to the Passover Lamb; for He, like water, went to the lowest place. We find Him when we do the same.

One key to managerial success is good subordinates. Is this principle verified in the case of the most successful manager and founder of the world's largest and longest-lasting business?

> MARK 14:18: "And as they were at table eating, Jesus said, 'Truly, I say to you, one of you will betray me.'"

This Host chose His own parasite as one of His guests. For His business was to be both kinds of Host.

Couldn't Hell be empty?

> MARK 14:21: "The Son of man goes as it is written
> of him, but woe to that man by whom the Son of
> man is betrayed! It would have been better for that
> man if he had not been born."

He would never say that of any of the Blessed in
Heaven. We need to know there is a lake of fire under
the world of time for the same reason skaters need to
know there is a lake of water under the thin ice.

*What one verse in the Bible do Fundamentalist literalists
never interpret literally?*

> MARK 14:22: "And as they were eating, he took
> bread, and blessed, and broke it, and gave it to them,
> and said, 'Take; this is my body.' "

Protestants and Catholics will never agree about what
this means until they agree that it is a mystery to be
lovingly explored rather than a problem to be curiously
solved.

*This world is a bloody mess. What solution do Christians
offer to clean it up?*

MARK 14:24: "And he said to them, 'This is my blood of the covenant, which is poured out for many.' "

Blood can be washed away by blood.

197

Will there be wine in Heaven?

MARK 14:25: "Truly, I say to you, I shall not drink again of the fruit of the vine until that day when I drink it new in the kingdom of God."

Jesus was neither a drunk nor a teetotaler. No Christians should be drunks, but some may be teetotalers.

198

What singing group performed before the greatest occasion in history?

MARK 14:26: "And when they had sung a hymn, they went out to the Mount of Olives [for Jesus to be captured and crucified]."

"The Apostles and the Master" sang "pre-Vatican II" hymns.

199

What percentage of (a) Christians, (b) saints, and (c) apostles obey the first and greatest commandment and would never deny or fall away from Christ?

MARK 14:27: "And Jesus said to them, 'You will all fall away.' "

The Great Commandment is not our *prescription*, for none of us can swallow it with whole heart and soul. It is our *X ray*, so that all of us know we are mortally ill and need the Great Physician.

200

When did a man beat a rooster in a crowing contest 3 to 2?

MARK 14:29–30: "Peter said to him, 'Even though they all fall away, I will not.' And Jesus said to him, 'Truly, I say to you, this very night, before the cock crows twice, you will deny me three times.' But he said vehemently, 'If I must die with you, I will not deny you.' "

The rooster crowed when the sun was coming up. Peter crowed when the Son was going down.

201

Is favoritism wrong? Should we treat everyone equally?

MARK 14:32–33: "And they went to a place which was called Gethsemane; and he said to his disciples, 'Sit here, while I pray.' And he took with him Peter and James and John."

Only three were taken to the heights (the Mount of Transfiguration) and to the depths, here. Only twelve were chosen to be apostles. Only one was chosen to be the rock. Friendship is deeper than equality. Equality is justice; friendship is love.

202

Is the fully enlightened consciousness of a "perfect master" above and free from sorrow, as Stoics and Buddhists say?

> MARK 14:34: "And he said to them, 'My soul is very sorrowful.' "

Emotions are like waves. Sentimentalists are like fish, who live in them. Stoics and Buddhists are like birds, who fly over them. Christ is like a surfer, who rides them.

203

How perfected and advanced in faith would you judge a man to be if his prayer were: "God, please get me out of this mess; I can't take it"?

> MARK 14:35: "And going a little farther, he fell on the ground and prayed that, if it were possible, the hour might pass from him."

"Help!" shows faith, not lack of faith.

204

If a Christian found Aladdin's lamp, with only one wish left, what would he wish for?

MARK 14:36: "And he said, 'Abba, Father, all things are possible to you; remove this chalice from me; yet not what I will, but what you will.'"

A Christian is not one who corrects Christ. Here is Christ's absolute.

205

What spiritual posture are we in most of the time?

MARK 14:37: "And he came and found them sleeping, and he said to Peter, 'Simon, are you asleep? Could you not watch one hour?'"

Who sleeps through both love and war? We do.

206

Among all the things that are in our power, what are our two strongest weapons against evil?

MARK 14:38: "Watch and pray that you may not enter into temptation."

Many watch but do not pray: those who are wise as serpents but not harmless as doves. Many pray but do not watch: those who are harmless as doves but not wise as serpents. Our Commander has given us our complete instructions, so that our watching mind may be one with our praying heart.

*According to the New Testament, if we are "born again",
we have two natures, two kinds of life: one from our parents,
and another from God. Is there any evidence in our ordinary
experience that this mystery is true?*

> MARK 14:38: "The spirit indeed is willing, but the
> flesh is weak."

The flesh is why we are not as good as we want to be.
The Spirit is why we want to be better than we are.
See Romans 7:15–20.

*Is it not in vain and a waste to say the same thing over and
over again when you pray?*

> MARK 14:39: "And again he went away and prayed,
> saying the same words."

Not all repetition is "vain repetition". Singers always
use repetition, whether they sing in happiness or in
sorrow. No one says "I love you" or "Help!" only
once.

*What will we answer God when He asks us why we failed
Him?*

> MARK 14:40: "And again he came and found them
> sleeping, for their eyes were very heavy; and they
> did not know what to answer him."

When we meet God, we must speak the truth. Often, the truth is silence.

210

My theology teacher interprets Jesus as a Marxist and the Gospel as an economic, political, and social "liberation". I keep falling asleep in his class. What would Jesus say to me?

MARK 14:41: "Are you still sleeping and taking your rest? It is enough; the hour has come; the Son of man is betrayed into the hands of sinners. Rise, let us be going; see, my betrayer is at hand."

Judas betrayed Jesus probably because Jesus did not fit his ideological agenda. Judas' successors are still working, with the same subtle kiss.

211

What is a theologian doing when he interprets Jesus in a worldly way, simply as "the man for others", not as God?

MARK 14:44: "Now the betrayer had given them a sign, saying, 'The one I shall kiss is the man; seize him and lead him away safely.'"

The de-clawing of Christ the Tiger by the worldly followers of Judas is the kiss of death.

212

What do we do when we use Christ's name to justify our personal expectations?

MARK 14:45: "And when he came, he [Judas] went up to him at once, and said, 'Master!' And he kissed him."

Not all who call Him "Master" are His servants.

The Hundred Years' War was the longest and bloodiest religious war in history. It ended in a complex compromise, the Treaty of Westphalia, after a horrible number of casualties. What was the shortest religious war in history, how did it end, and how many casualties did it have?

MARK 14:46–47: "And they laid hands on him and seized him. But one of those who stood by drew his sword, and struck the slave of the high priest and cut off his ear."

Luke 22:50–51 and John 18:10–11 tell how this war ended.

What would Jesus say to preachers who think they have Him all figured out?

MARK 14:49: "Day after day I was with you in the temple teaching, and you did not seize me."

We do not seize the Word in our net of words. The Fisher of men is not a fish to be caught in men's nets.

What road map through life did Jesus follow?

MARK 14:49: "Let the Scriptures be fulfilled."

The House obeyed the blueprint. The Word fulfilled the Word.

216

Why was Job a greater saint than any of the apostles?

MARK 14:50: "And they all deserted him and fled."

Job never did that, even though he had better reason to.

217

Who invented "streaking"?

MARK 14:51–52: "And a young man followed him, with nothing but a linen cloth about his body; and they seized him, but he left the linen cloth and ran away naked."

His body showed what our souls all are to God.

218

How do Christians usually follow Christ?

MARK 14:54: "And Peter had followed him at a distance, right into the courtyard of the high priest."

It is extremely dangerous to get close to Him. Those who do always share His sufferings. They also share His joys. His sufferings are finite; His joys are infinite.

219

What is the consensus of the world's minds about Jesus?

> MARK 14:56: "For many bore false witness against him, and their witness did not agree."

Recipe for Babel: "truth" by consensus.

220

Many martyrs have made great speeches to defend themselves before they die; for instance, Socrates' Apology. *What is the greatest difference between all of them and Jesus' defense at His trial?*

> MARK 14:60–61: "And the high priest stood up in their midst, and asked Jesus, 'Have you no answer to make? What is it that these men testify against you?' But he was silent and made no answer."

To answer at all would be to answer falsely, for He is not the answerer, but the Questioner; not the man judged, but the Judge of man.

Who first came up with the idea that Jesus was divine?

> MARK 14:61–62: "Again the high priest asked him,
> 'Are you the Christ, the Son of the Blessed?' And
> Jesus said, 'I am; and you will see the Son of man
> sitting at the right hand of Power, and coming with
> the clouds of heaven.'"

That is so clear that only a scholar could possibly miss
it.

If Jesus was only a man, what kind of man was He?

> MARK 14:63–64 [see no. 221 first]: "And the high
> priest tore his clothes, and said, 'Why do we still
> need witnesses? You have heard his blasphemy. What
> is your decision?' And they all condemned him as
> deserving death."

If Jesus was not the Lord of life, then no one ever de-
served death more than He, the biggest blasphemer in
history.

*What sort of worship did the world give to God when He
revealed Himself most completely?*

> MARK 14:65: "And some began to spit on him, and
> to cover his face, and to strike him."

If God revealed Himself even more completely and explicitly than He did in Jesus, if that were possible, the world would also reveal *itself* more explicitly than it did to Jesus.

224

Like children, we cry a lot over trivia: when our toys fail to function or when we get a boo-boo. Death, however, rightly elicits tears; Christ Himself wept over His friend Lazarus' death (Jn 11:33–35). Is there anything that even more rightly elicits weeping than death? Is there anything worse than death?

MARK 14:66–72: "And as Peter was below in the courtyard, one of the maids of the high priest came; and seeing Peter warming himself, she looked at him, and said, 'You also were with the Nazarene, Jesus.' But he denied it, saying, 'I neither know nor understand what you mean.' And he went out into the gateway. And the maid saw him, and began again to say to the bystanders, 'This man is one of them.' But again he denied it. And after a little while again the bystanders said to Peter, 'Certainly you are one of them; for you are a Galilean.' But he began to invoke a curse on himself and to swear, 'I do not know this man of whom you speak.' And immediately the cock crowed a second time. And Peter remembered how Jesus had said to him, 'Before the cock crows twice, you will deny me three times.' And he broke down and wept."

Sin is worse than death. Peter wept wisely. Saints weep often.

225

Are committees necessarily more wise and just than dictators? What would a committee have done to Jesus?

> MARK 15:1: "And as soon as it was morning the chief priests, with the elders and scribes, and the whole council held a consultation; and they bound Jesus and led him away and delivered him to Pilate."

This was not the last time that happened.

226

What is the best answer to an ambiguous question?

> MARK 15:2-3: "And Pilate asked him, 'Are you the King of the Jews?' And he answered him, 'You have said so.'"

An unambiguous answer to an ambiguous question would buy into the question's ambiguity; only an ambiguous answer escapes it. Therefore, only an ambiguous answer avoids ambiguity.

227

What can a Christian say to make a skeptical, bored, jaded, worldly mind that has "heard it all before" sit up and take notice and wonder?

MARK 15:5: "But Jesus made no further answer, so that Pilate wondered."

Sometimes silence shouts.

228

What kind of a world would we have if democracy reigned everywhere and the people ruled?

MARK 15:6–15: "Now at the feast he used to release for them one prisoner for whom they asked. And among the rebels in prison, who had committed murder in the insurrection, there was a man called Barabbas. And the crowd came up and began to ask Pilate to do as he always did for them. And he answered them, 'Do you want me to release for you the King of the Jews?' For he perceived that it was out of envy that the chief priests had delivered him up. But the chief priests stirred up the crowd to have him release for them Barabbas instead. And Pilate again said to them, 'Then what shall I do with the man whom you call the King of the Jews?' And they cried out again, 'Crucify him.' And Pilate said to them, 'Why, what evil has he done?' But they shouted all the more, 'Crucify him.' So Pilate, wishing to satisfy the crowd, released for them Barabbas; and having scourged Jesus, he delivered him to be crucified."

Precisely because people are equal, because rulers are no better than the people, therefore the people are no better than the rulers.

With what character in the Gospels would a Christian most perfectly identify?

MARK 15:15: "Pilate . . . released . . . Barabbas; and . . . delivered [Jesus] to be crucified."

Jesus was delivered to death to deliver Barabbas and his ilk from death. Christians are Barabbas' ilk.

The title "Christ the King" seems wrong and unfit for a democratic, anti-authoritarian age. What kind of king is He? What is He king of? It sounds suspiciously triumphalist and militaristic.

MARK 15:16–18: "And the soldiers led him away inside the palace (that is, the praetorium); and they called together the whole battalion. And they clothed him in a purple [royal] cloak, and plaiting a crown of thorns they put it on him. And they began to salute him, 'Hail, King of the Jews!' "

His cloak was lordly but fake. His crown was un-lordly but true.

Clergy, judges, and soldiers seem to be the three professions that are entrusted with preserving righteousness, justice, and honor in every society. How did they act at the most crucial and revealing occasion in history?

(A) MARK 15:10: "It was out of envy that the chief priests had delivered him up."

(B) MARK 15:14-15: "And Pilate said to them, 'Why, what evil has he done?' But they shouted all the more, 'Crucify him.' So Pilate, wishing to satisfy the crowd, released for them Barabbas; and having scourged Jesus, he delivered him to be crucified."

(C) MARK 15:16-20: "And the soldiers . . . clothed him in a purple cloak, and plaiting a crown of thorns they put it on him. And they began to salute him, 'Hail, King of the Jews!' And they struck his head with a reed, and spat upon him, and they knelt down in homage to him. And when they had mocked him, they stripped him of the purple cloak, and put his own clothes on him. And they led him out to crucify him."

When the chips are down, the uniforms come off.

232

Can anyone do a good deed under compulsion?

MARK 15:21: "And they compelled a passer-by, Simon of Cyrene, who was coming in from the country, the father of Alexander and Rufus, to carry his cross."

Do you think the martyrs *volunteered* for martyrdom? That would not be martyrdom but suicide. Or do you think their deed of martyrdom was not a good deed? Many good deeds are done under compulsion.

Many "primitive" peoples believe that their place of worship is "the navel of the earth", the center of the cosmos, "the still point of the turning world". Is there any truth to this myth? Is there really such a place, a hub around which all the wheel of time and history turns? If so, what does it look like?

MARK 15:22−24: "And they brought him to the place called Golgotha (which means the place of a skull). . . . And they crucified him."

In the navel of Mother Earth, there is a skull. At the heart of life, there is death. Because of that death, at the heart of death there is life.

Most technological inventions can be used for either good or evil. But isn't the invention of anesthetics simply good? Isn't the relief of suffering a universal moral good?

MARK 15:23: "And they offered him wine mingled with myrrh; but he did not take it."

The modern world is full of anesthetics, for souls as well as bodies.

Summarize the history of Christian theology for the last five hundred years.

MARK 15:24: "And they crucified him, and divided his garments among them, casting lots for them, to decide what each should take."

But His royal robe was seamless. There must be some truth everywhere, but there must also be all truth somewhere.

236

Of what charge was Jesus actually guilty? (Hint: the charge was written down for all to see.)

MARK 15:26: "And the inscription of the charge against him read, 'The King of the Jews.'"

He was indeed the King of the Jews. The Jews were the "chosen people", and they were chosen to suffer, and He was the King of Suffering.

237

With what kind of people was Christ surrounded in life and death?

MARK 15:27: "And with him they crucified two robbers."

There *are* no other kind of people.

238

How would you characterize the ideologies of the Right and the Left vis-à-vis Christ?

MARK 15:27: ". . . two robbers, one on his right and one on his left."

Those on the Right rob Him of His heart, and those on the Left rob Him of His head (His mind, His words, His headship). To be to the Right of Christ is *not* to be right. To be to the Left of Christ is to be left.

239

Modern man lives like a dog, wagging his tail; i.e., he is hedonistic and sexually provocative. Is there any worse way to live than this?

MARK 15:29: "And those who passed by derided him, shaking [KJV: wagging] their heads, and saying, 'Aha! You who would destroy the temple and build it in three days, save yourself, and come down from the cross!'"

Wagging your head is worse than wagging your tail. Publicans wag their tails; Pharisees wag their heads. Wagging your tail makes you like a dog; wagging your head makes you like a devil. No sin is lower than a sneer.

240

Jesus is the Savior of all men. Is there any man Jesus could not save?

MARK 15:31: "He saved others; he cannot save himself."

It was meant as a taunt, but it was a truth. If He had saved Himself, He could not have saved others.

What do unbelievers demand before they will believe? What deters them from faith? What conditions do they put on faith that Jesus, faith's object, does not fulfill?

> MARK 15:32: "Let the Christ, the King of Israel, come down now from the cross, that we may see and believe."

An Easter without a Good Friday, a Christ without a Cross, a Heaven without a Hell, is what they want. But what they want does not exist.

Did Hell ever come to earth? If so, what did it look like?

> MARK 15:33: "And when the sixth hour had come, there was darkness over the whole land until the ninth hour."

Heaven is like the sun, conquering the darkness by sharing its light.

Hell is like a Black Hole, sucking light into its own inner emptiness.

Hell looks like Nothing.

Did anyone ever hear *Hell on earth? If so, what did it sound like?*

> MARK 15:34: "And at the ninth hour Jesus cried with a loud voice, 'Eloi, Eloi, lama sabachthani?' which means, 'My God, my God, why have you forsaken me?'"

Angels dared not hear, angels could not endure, the words we heard, when God was forsaken by God.

What did Jesus say that we will never say in all eternity?

> MARK 15:34: "My God, my God, why have you forsaken me?"

If He had not said this in time, we would say it in eternity.

Who showed up when no one but Jesus expected him, to see the brightest light ever seen on earth, but did not *show up when everyone but Jesus* did *expect him, to see the greatest darkness ever seen on earth?*

> MARK 9:2–4: "And after six days Jesus took with him Peter and James and John, and led them up

a high mountain apart by themselves; and he was transfigured before them, and his garments became glistening, intensely white, as no fuller on earth could bleach them. And there appeared to them Elijah with Moses; and they were talking to Jesus."

MARK 15:34–36: "And at the ninth hour Jesus cried with a loud voice, 'Eloi, Eloi, lama sabachthani?' which means, 'My God, my God, why have you forsaken me?' And some of the bystanders hearing it said, 'Behold, he is calling Elijah. . . . Wait, let us see whether Elijah will come to take him down.' "

One who goes to Heaven in a chariot of fire can be expected to show up at unexpected times and places.

246

A wise man's last words should reveal the nature of death. What was Jesus' very last word, spoken with His very last breath?

MARK 15:37: "And Jesus uttered a loud cry, and breathed his last."

Everything Jesus said and did reveals truth. Nothing is accidental. The horror of death is its wordless cry. The Word shared also this wordlessness.

247

A God we can reach is not worth reaching; but a God worth reaching is not one we can reach. "You can't get there from here." There are two infinite distances separating us: the infinite distance between Creator and creature, and the infinitely more infinite distance between holiness and sin. How does Christianity untie this Gordian knot?

> MARK 15:38: "And the curtain of the temple [surrounding the Holy of Holies, where God alone dwelt] was torn in two, from top to bottom."

The Gordian knot was not untied but cut with a sword. A problem impossible to solve in thought may be solved in act.

248

What miracle could convert a hard-hearted professional killer?

> MARK 15:39: "And when the centurion, who stood facing him, saw that he thus breathed his last, he said, 'Truly this man was the Son of God!'"

Hard hearts are softened by softness, not hardness; by failure, not by success; by weakness, not by power.

249

Everyone shows his true color in the light of Jesus, especially when the chips are down. Did women show themselves to be "the weaker sex", as men have often called them, around Jesus?

> MARK 15:40–41: "There were also women looking on from afar, among whom were Mary Magdalene,

and Mary the mother of James the younger and of Joses, and Salome, who, when he was in Galilee, followed him, and ministered to him; and also many other women who came up with him to Jerusalem."

The apostles, meanwhile, had run away.

250

Couldn't Jesus have only fainted and then recovered and escaped, rather than really dying and rising from the dead?

MARK 15:44–46: "And Pilate wondered if he were already dead; and summoning the centurion, he asked him whether he was already dead. And when he learned from the centurion that he was dead, he granted the body to Joseph. And he bought a linen shroud, and taking him down, wrapped him in the linen shroud, and laid him in a tomb which had been hewn out of the rock; and he rolled a stone against the door of the tomb."

Figure it out for yourself.